Historical Association Studies

The French Reformation

Mark Greengrass

Historical Association Studies
General Editors: Roger Mettam and James Shields

Decolonization
The Fall of the European Empires
M. E. Chamberlain

Gandhi
Antony Copley

The Counter-Reformation
N. S. Davidson

British Radicalism and the French Revolution
1789–1815
H. T. Dickinson

From Luddism to the First Reform Bill
Reform in England 1810–1832
J. R. Dinwiddy

Radicalism in the English Revolution 1640–1660
F. D. Dow

The French Reformation
Mark Greengrass

Politics in the Reign of Charles II
K. H. D. Haley

Occupied France
Collaboration and Resistance 1940–1944
H. R. Kedward

Britain's Decline
Problems and Perspectives
Alan Sked

Bismarck
Bruce Waller

The Historical Association, 59a Kennington Park Road, London SE11 4JH

The French Reformation

MARK GREENGRASS

Basil Blackwell

Copyright © Mark Greengrass 1987

First published 1987

Basil Blackwell Ltd
108 Cowley Road, Oxford, OX4 1JF, UK

Basil Blackwell Inc.
432 Park Avenue South, Suite 1503
New York, NY 10016, USA

British Library Cataloguing in Publication Data

Greengrass, Mark
 The French Reformation. —— (Historical Association studies)
 1. Reformation —— France
 I. Title   II. Series
 274.4'06   BR370
 ISBN 0-631-14516-8

Library of Congress Cataloging in Publication Data

 Greengrass, M.
 The French Reformation.
 (Historical Association studies)
 Bibliography: p.
 Includes index.
 1. Reformation —— France. 2. Protestant churches —— France ——
History —— 16th century. 3. France —— History ——Wars of the Huguenots,
1562–1598. 4. France —— Church history —— 16th century. I. Title.
II. Series.
BR370.G74 1987   274.4'06   86–21541
ISBN 0-631-14516-8 (pbk.)

Typeset in 10½ on 11½ point Baskerville
by Photo-Graphics, Honiton, Devon
Printed in Great Britain by Page Bros (Norwich) Ltd

Contents

Preface

'There are no more glorious pages in the history of humanity than those of the French Reformation' said the president of the newly formed Society for the History of French Protestantism (*Société de l'Histoire du Protestantisme Français*) in his inaugural lecture of 1853 (Nicholls, 1984, p. 26). His lavish sentiments were often reflected in the course of the next 50 years in the pages of the Bulletin of the society. In the space not devoted to edited documents, the Bulletin presented an inevitably positive picture of the French reformation for the faithful. It was doctrinally united around Calvinism. It was a struggle for liberty and progress and not just an accident occasioned by the abuses in the traditional church. Protestants were also good Frenchmen, enlightened citizens, rarely intolerant and never seditious demagogues.

The need to present the history of the French reformation to the faithful as a kind of witness to truth despite persecution is understandable, given the shape of the French protestant past. But it lasted long after professional historical enquiry made it look anachronistic, partly because of the religious controversies which dominated French life before the First World War. Protestants had to endure, in the epoch of the Dreyfus affair, the odious and contradictory criticisms of the clerical Right Wing which portrayed them – with the Jews and Freemasons – as the begetters of capitalism, socialism and immorality. The efforts of the great French educational reformer, Jules Ferry, were described in hostile clerical quarters as 'the revenge of the reformation'. No study of the French reformation can begin without being aware of the longstanding lack of national consensus about the significance of the reformation in French life.

Gradually, the crucial elements in the debate about the French reformation have been reformulated by French professional or academic historians. We shall be referring in these pages to the fundamental works of Imbart de la Tour, Henri Hauser, Lucien Romier, Lucien Febvre and Janine Garrisson. Even the old chronology – what Lucien Febvre once caricatured as the inevitable tragedy in three acts (pre-reform, reform and counter-reform) – has to be abandoned. Historians are now more aware of the social and cultural problems raised by the French reformation as well as its regional diversities, and these are reflected in the pages which follow. Nineteenth-century historians were obsessed with the origins of the reformation; we shall be more interested in its course and impact.

I am grateful to Professors Francis Higman, Robert Knecht and Dr David Nicholls for answering individual queries and to Dr Joe Bergin for his careful reading of the early draft. In a text written for students, it is appropriate that it should be dedicated to the students of the university of Pau in session 1985–6 who were unwitting 'cobayes' to many of its pages, as well as to Mark Bosworth and François Head who persuaded me in the nicest way that it needed to be written.

Finally, I should explain the significance of the illustration that appears on the cover of the book. The message round the emblem recalls the remark by Calvin to the King of Navarre, Antoine de Bourbon, after the massacre of Vassy in 1562: 'It is in truth for God's Church, in whose name I speak, to endure blows and not to strike them. Remember, though, that this is an anvil which has broken many a hammer before now.'

1 Heterodoxy in the Early French Reformation

'Everyone has his own opinion'; this was the impression left on Boniface Amerbach, a student from Basle at the university of Avignon in the early 1520s, by the lack of orthodoxy that he had discovered in this papal sovereign enclave within France. He had done more than his fair share to add to it, since he was a supporter of the 'Excellent Doctor Martin' (Luther), and sought news and pamphlets of the German and Swiss reformers from Johann Froben in Basle (Luther's publisher), to pass on to his eager friends in Avignon. The French reformation begins with what the historian Lucien Febvre described as 'a long period of magnificent religious anarchy' (Febvre, 1969, p. 68).

This anarchy – heterodoxy is perhaps a better word since the most anarchic part of the continental reformation, anabaptism, hardly made a showing at all in France – was by no means confined to France, nor had it necessarily begun with the protestant reformation. Its existence should occasion no surprise when the universal church claimed an eternal authority and an exclusive preserve over truth, still less when the multiplicity of functions which it had gradually assumed in the course of the previous three centuries is taken into account. The church baptized, educated, married, dispensed to the poor, administered to the prince, protected society against what it chose to define as the enemies of the human race, authorized penance, excommunicated and acted as an advocate with a God whose judgement without the mediation of the church was thought to be too terrible. At every rite of passage, the church was the critical social organism, delineating the good from the evil, linking the quick with the dead and the yet unborn. Furthermore, these heavy tasks assumed

1

a level of training, especially among the secular clergy, which neither the episcopacy nor the papacy had ever provided. The result was a clergy which was hugely divided between an aristocracy of the well-educated, well-beneficed and trained, and a clerical proletariat. There were, of course, bureaucratic ways of ensuring that the church carried out its mission. The labyrinth of canon law, the machinery of church courts, dispensations and diocesan visitations, not to mention purgatory and its associated spiritual ministration, were there in part to fulfil that function; but it was also probably the case that, when faced with new heterodoxy, this bureaucracy made the church less adaptable and capable of championing its orthodoxy.

The French church was, in these respects, little different from others in Europe. Its ecclesiastical establishment was powerful, privileged and well established, a reflection of the enormous prestige and influence it had enjoyed during the Middle Ages. There were 114 French bishoprics and archbishoprics, organized into 14 provinces with a parochial structure which enveloped the traditional rural communities of France. No one knew how many parishes there really were in the realm, but the best contemporary estimates put it at about 32,000. In addition, France boasted some of the most distinguished monastic establishments of the Middle Ages such as Cluny, Cîteaux, Prémontré, Fontevrault and La Chaise-Dieu. Among its 13 universities, it counted the faculty of theology in Paris (known as the Sorbonne) which was among the most respected in Europe, and this was why Martin Luther agreed to submit his theological works to its scrutiny in 1519, and why, later, Henry VIII sought a favourable ruling on the legitimacy of his divorce from its learned doctors.

The prestige of the upper echelons of the clergy was huge. Archbishops and bishops were often temporal lords as well as spiritual ones. In the 23 ecclesiastical dioceses of Languedoc, one of the largest French provinces of the Midi, the archbishop of Narbonne and the bishops of Albi, Alais, Castres, Lodève, St Papoul and Uzès, were seigneurs of extensive noble estates. The province's bishops dispensed secular justice and were concerned with the collection of royal tax. Languedoc's bishops in the first generation of the protestant reformation followed an established pattern. Some were Italians; dynasties like the Medici, Bonzi or Rucellai had, with royal support, rooted themselves in the Midi dioceses like elm trees in a drain. Others were French royal nominees and clients of the king, such as Guillaume Pellicier, bishop of Montpellier, a French ambassador and a noted scholar and humanist, or his successor in the see, Antoine Sujet, king's musician and the descendant of a family of civil servants. These figures rarely came from the province where they served; they were obvious newcomers, representing royal power in church and state, a sign of a patronage which French kings had exercised *de facto* from the fifteenth century, but which had been legalized by the famous agreement between the pope and Francis I in 1516, the Concordat of Bologna. But these by no means eliminated the scions of noble clans of the province, whose families had exploited the local bishopric as a kind of dynastic inheritance for generations. The Polignac family at Le Puy and the Lévis-Mirepoix at Lodève are but two examples of provincial baronial clans which used bishoprics in a patrimonial way. Those which had been temporarily ousted by royal nominees still sought ways of reinstalling themselves in order to exploit the property, privilege and rights which they regarded as properly theirs.

In the cities (most sizeable towns in France were episcopal sees, and those which were not generally had a collegial church with resident canons), the clerical presence was felt particularly through the cathedral canons. Nearly 90 in Toulouse, over 100 in Narbonne (the numbers are difficult to establish precisely), they were generally from the families of the notables of the city. In Toulouse, they were often relatives of judges in the sovereign court of the province, the *parlement*, and one or two sat in the court as judges themselves. In Lyon, the 32 canon counts of the chapter of St John were required to be of French noble ancestry for at least four generations and they were drawn from the great noble families of the region. These connections were encouraged and protected by a system of dispensations known by its Latin name, *resignatio in favorem*, whereby a canon could resign his post to a member of his family or any nominee of his choice. A similar arrangement was in the process of being adopted with royal offices on the eve of the reformation, with the addition of the actual sale of the office. It was formally forbidden to sell ecclesiastical positions but the protestants were not the first to signal the widespread existence of simony (the sale of ecclesiastical benefices) for what were both sought after and privileged posts. The cathedrals in which the canons had their stalls had changed little since the high Middle Ages. In Lyon, for example, no organ was allowed, little preaching was encouraged and the three lay confraternities whose presence was tolerated within the cathedral were required to leave their banners in the porch. The cathedral was, in short, a rich reliquary, like the silver casket, decorated with gold, pearls and pieces of the holy cross which held the jaw of St John the Baptist and which was the canon counts' prize exhibit in their relic collection.

The senior clergy rarely preached and was often, because of the cumulation of benefices, non-resident. The performance of parochial tasks was assigned to vicars who had been ordained as priests but who had no benefice. Becoming a member of the clergy was not difficult in sixteenth-century France. The tonsure was easily acquired; bishops tonsured individuals on their episcopal visitations as they might confirm children. Thereafter, they might enter one of the regular orders which would present them for ordination in due course or, more commonly, they would beg, borrow and steal their way to a diocese like Avignon, where ordinations were available even to strangers of the diocese from suffragan bishops who accepted dispensations for those who were under age, unqualified or otherwise unsuitable. From the upland regions where the traditions of migration into the church were strong but education was weak, they came in large numbers: 534 were ordained in the diocese of Avignon in 1532, 162 in nearby Orange in 1514, a remarkable 1,096 in the otherwise undistinguished Normandy diocese of Séez in 1514. They then undertook the often itinerant life of the poor *clericus*, enjoying exemption from taxation and criminal prosecution in the civil courts, but otherwise virtually indistinguishable from vagabond classes of early sixteenth-century France (Venard, 1968, pp. 987–1016; Rapp, 1971, p. 213). In Toulouse, an average of four priests were assaulted each month in the year 1499–1500, a measure not just of a widespread anticlericalism but also of a disordered clerical underworld (Mirouse, 1984, p. 59).

4

Monumental resources had been invested during the Middle Ages by both church and state to secure doctrinal unity, and superficially this seemed to have been successful. Nowhere was this more so than in France, 'the purest and most prosperous part of Christendom' and the only country free from heresy, as Erasmus described it in 1517 (Mann, 1934, p. 22). The Cathars, the most serious heretical group to confront the medieval church, were defeated in southern France in the thirteenth century. An inquisition was developed with the collaboration of the kings of France to stamp out its embers. A similar cooperation between the forces of church and state seemed, in the late fifteenth and early sixteenth century, to be about to wipe out the malevolent presence of witchcraft too.

In reality, heterodoxy could survive as the Waldensians (*Vaudois*) in Dauphiné, Provence and the Comtat Venaissin demonstrated. These were migrant communities from the Alpine areas of Piedmont which had settled in the valleys on the French side of the Alps, with which they had close contacts through their pastoral farming, and in the regions adjacent where there was room after the Black Death for more systematic colonization. They were never very numerous – contemporaries spoke of about 6,000 Waldensians in Provence in the early 1530s – but, as was to be expected in the circumstances, they upheld their distinctive traditions in the first generations, sustained in their closed communities by high levels of inter-marriage and the custom of placing leadership in the hands of certain families. Whether their distinctive religious traditions were really as heretical as they struck the inquisitors (and inquisitorial documents are all that historians have to rely on here) is a matter for debate. It has recently been argued that Waldensian beliefs were sustained not so much by their 'barbes', or 'oncles' – itinerant Holy Men, perhaps on a Franciscan model – but by a kind of rural proverbial wisdom which was handed down from generation to generation and which expressed the essence of Waldensian beliefs in a simple form which fitted admirably their rural and isolated existence (Cameron, 1984, chs iv–ix). To a hostile inquisitor, these heterodox proverbs could be presented

5

as deeply heretical in a way which perhaps was not intended. Sayings like, 'You can only go to Heaven or Hell', 'You may as well be buried in a field as a cemetery', 'Better to be shriven by a worthy man than by a worthless priest', may have been relatively innocuous, if heterodox, statements to those in communities where the presence of the Catholic church was not heavily felt, but to the hostile inquisitor they seemed deeply heretical, denying the existence of purgatory and the saving power of the church, and therefore deserving of persecution. Protestant apologists, looking back from the sixteenth century, were keen to see the 'Waldenses' (as they called them) as the direct ancestors of the French reform, spiritual brethren in their beliefs and opposition to the traditional church. In fact, the protestant ministers who were sent later in the 1550s to infiltrate Waldensian communities found it no easier to enforce their severely rational protestant theology on these rural communities than on any others. To the Waldensians, the protestant ministers seemed more akin to the old priests in their desire to seize power in their communities, than to the 'barbes' who had supported the Waldensian village fathers who customarily exercised it.

The persecution, having been sporadic in the early fifteenth century, reached a dramatic peak in Dauphiné in the spring of 1487 with a crusade against the Waldensians in which many were summarily tried (often with the use of extortion and threats of torture) and their property and goods seized while many others fled to Provence and the Comtat. The incident is important for historians since it gives us an opportunity to measure the effectiveness of the inquisition in the generation before the reformation in France (Cameron, 1984, chs ii–iii). There is more than a suggestion that this crusade was a vehicle for some pretty unscrupulous lawyers with the encouragement of the local gentry to confiscate the migrants' wealth, rather than save their souls. Another of their proverbs ran ruefully that 'their heresy was in their wallets and if they had been poor, they would never have been accused of such things.' The leaders of the Waldensian villages were, however, able to raise funds to pay the legal costs of an appeal to the royal courts and it was these efforts which led to their partial rehabilitation by royal justice in 1509. Far from eliminating the Waldensians, this crusade scattered their communities more widely and tended to confirm the suspicions in the minds of secular lawyers that the Inquisition, and that kind of legal enforcement of religious orthodoxy generally, was untrustworthy and required very strict surveillance by the state.

Erasmus may be forgiven, however, for having misinterpreted the size of the machinery enforcing orthodoxy in France on the eve of the reform as an indication of its effectiveness. The Sorbonne, the bishops, the king, the 'sovereign' law courts, the town councils all had duties in this direction, and there was always a risk of their treading on each other's toes as they tried to undertake the task. More importantly, none of them was particularly well equipped for dealing with the newer conditions created in Renaissance Europe which allowed heresy to flourish. Among these the most important in France and Europe were the printing presses and the cities.

The power of the new printing presses to propagate dissent beyond the traditional boundaries of the Middle Ages was unparalleled and there were no coherent mechanisms readily to hand for either controlling or exploiting it. France was initially somewhat behind its near neighbours in the growth of printing, doubtless because of the retarding effects of the Hundred Years War. In 1480, there were only 8 or 9 centres of printing in France compared with about 50 in Italy and 48 in the Low Countries and Germany, mainly in the Rhineland to the north and east of France. By 1500, however, France was catching up fast. Over 40 towns had flourishing presses and a number of itinerant printers moved round the Midi where facilities were not extensive (Febvre and Martin, 1976, pp. 182–3; Martin and Chartier, 1982, p. 174). Only 550 works were published in England between 1520 and 1529, whereas in Paris alone the number produced in one year (1530) was nearly 300 which made it, by this date, the rival to the market leaders Antwerp and Venice. But one result of the intensity of this growth was that the learned in France became subjected to two separate, but powerful and coordinating, intellectual movements. From the cities and presses of Italy came the movement to revive antique pre-Christian culture, as interpreted and expressed in Italian humanist circles and known as the Renaissance. From the cities and presses of the Rhineland came another intellectual current

7

known as the 'Modern Devotion' (*Devotio Moderna*), a movement for individual, lay spiritual renewal based on powerful new techniques of silent prayer and contemplation and expressed in movements such as the Brethren of the Common Life. Hence, in Paris in the years before the reformation, among the books printed were, on the one hand, Thomas à Kempis' *Imitation of Christ* and books by the more mystical of the Fathers (St Augustine, St Bernard) and, on the other, the works of classical literature, particularly of Seneca and Cicero, which found a ready market. But neither was as large as the market for traditional popular religious themes, such as the lives of the saints or the contemplations on death. According to a famous thesis by the French historian Augustin Renaudet, the fusing of the Renaissance and the Modern Devotion in Paris in the generation before 1520 created what he somewhat confusingly dubbed the 'pre-reform' (Renaudet, 1953). The term is no longer in common currency among historians, but all the evidence points to the fact that there was in Paris and other intellectual centres in France on the eve of the reform enough of an amalgam to question traditional Christianity in both its theological modes, and its concrete manifestations. The ecclesiastical authorities in France – as in Europe at large – did not oppose the printing press; the first in France operated from the cellars of the Sorbonne, and bishops encouraged the publication of works, including Holy Scripture, for the use of the learned. Nor did they set their faces against Italian humanism or Rhineland mysticism. They may be forgiven for failing to see the dangers for traditional Christianity in what must have appeared like powerful currents of renewal.

The printing presses were the embodiment of the wealth, power and pretensions of Europe's cities. If the defeat of a minority of rural and largely illiterate Waldensians did not prove easy, the enforcement of orthodoxy in these increasingly literate conurbations by traditional means was next to impossible. The city magistrates were themselves thoughtfully critical of ecclesiastical pretensions. Education, poverty, disease and crime were their problems and, when the church seemed incapable of offering new initiatives, they set about organizing their own. French cities were perhaps a little behind their European counterparts in this respect. But in Lyon, for example, a group of enlightened laity, with the help of a minority of clergy whose heterodoxy already made them suspect to their more conservative colleagues, cooperated to found a new general hospital for the poor, which opened its doors in 1534 and was the model for similar efforts in other towns (Davis, 1975, ch. ii). There was also a widespread movement to establish municipal colleges (roughly the equivalent of secondary schools) which were often in competition with the cathedral or choir schools. They gradually adopted the curriculum of the arts colleges of the university of Paris in which piety and rhetoric were both of importance (Huppert, 1984, chs iii–v). Protected by the magistrates, it would have been impossible, even if it had seemed desirable, to stifle the powerful heterodox currents at work in France's cities on the eve of reform.

Lutheranism and Heresy

It was the case, of course, that the explosion of the reformation in Germany could not fail, eventually, to clarify what was and was not heresy in France. After deliberating for some two years, the Sorbonne declared – more or less to coincide with the Diet of Worms – that 104 of Luther's theological propositions were heretical. The language used by the faculty of theology was uncompromising – he was accused of godless arrogance and of being the lackey of the devil. In 1523, Lutheran books were seized from a notable Parisian man of letters, Louis de Berquin (c.1490–1529), by the *parlement* of Paris and, at the same time, Lutheran literature on sale from booksellers was seized. Two years later, the queen mother and regent of France during the imprisonment of the king after his defeat at Pavia, ordered the extirpation of the 'evil and damnable sect and heresy of Luther' from the realm. The Sorbonne decreed, and the *parlement* confirmed, that all translations of Scripture should be suppressed and four senior judges were appointed to investigate a potential nest of heresy in the diocese of Meaux. Early in the following year, on 5 February 1526, the first list of forbidden Lutheran doctrines was issued by the *parlement*. The first burning for protestant heresy reported in the martyrology for France of Jean Crespin was of a modest weaver from Meaux in 1524. In 1529 the

Sorbonne claimed its first major victim, when the scholar and gentleman Louis de Berquin mounted the scaffold in the *place* Maubert for refusing to recant his heretical writings. In some provinces, the progress of heresy, and the first signs of its repression, were not far behind that of Paris. In Normandy, the first burnings of those whom historians have assumed to be Lutherans occurred in 1526. By 1530, the Strasbourg reformer Martin Bucer described the Norman Vexin as a 'little Germany'.

The clarity between orthodoxy and heresy was, however, a long way off, even in 1530. The impression of measured coherence in the institutional response to the Lutheran reform is almost completely illusory. Even the Sorbonne was bitterly divided and obsessed with the possibility of heresy in its ranks. Open discussions at faculty meetings threw doubts on the orthodoxy of at least 15 of its learned doctors, who never numbered more than 80 (Higman, 1979, chs i–ii; Farge, 1985). In January 1525, the complaint was heard that 'many of the *magistri* are said to be Lutherans and to favour the hated sect and to reveal the secrets of the Faculty ...' In any case, recommendations from the Sorbonne were often greeted in the 1520s and 1530s with considerable scepticism or ignored by the judges in Paris. Even when the *parlement* did act on the decisions of the Sorbonne, it could find its decision reversed by the desire of the king to protect his own clients and those of courtiers who enjoyed his favour. Louis de Berquin benefited in 1523 from such royal favour; in 1529 he was not so fortunate. There was still plenty of room to exploit the various conflicts of jurisdiction to good advantage.

Neither king nor judges wished, of course, to be thought of as condoning heresy; Francis I took his coronation oath to defend the faith seriously and the *parlements* were aware of the connections between the maintenance of the true religion and the upholding of the law (Knecht, 1978, pp. 157–222). The debate was over who was to define heresy and how seriously it was to be judged. Inevitably, both parties tended to see the matter in terms of the need to preserve public peace and prevent scandal. If either were threatened, then they generally demanded an exemplary and harsh repression in order to discourage others; but these short, sharp shocks rarely lasted long, and so the impression of inconsistency was reinforced.

dangers and slowness of translating and publishing reformed literature for the French market in the years before 1540, protestantism, in its looser and specifically French 'evangelical' context, had made considerable strides.

Briçonnet, Lefèvre d'Etaples and Marguerite of Navarre

In retrospect, it must have seemed to many French protestants that the days of 'magnificent religious anarchy' had been a mixed blessing; so many opportunities for evangelism had existed but the lack of a pre-eminent leader had left them powerless to exploit them. Theodore Beza (Théodore de Bèze, 1519–1605) reflected in his *Icones* of 1580 that 'France might have had another Luther in Louis de Berquin' and this was perhaps the case (Mann, 1934, p. 114); Berquin had the right qualifications in terms of education, background and friends. But the five years of conflict with the *parlement* and the Sorbonne in Paris gradually wore him down. The fact of the matter was that the heterodox conditions of the early French reform were not favourable to producing the kind of leadership which would be appropriate for the organized churches later on and so it was pointless to look for it. We may illustrate the point by examining the careers of three individuals at the emotional heart of the early French reformation; Guillaume Briçonnet, bishop of Meaux, the scholar Jacques Lefèvre d'Etaples, and the king's sister, Marguerite d'Angoulême.

Briçonnet (c.1472–1534) was the son of a family from the Loire valley which knew the corridors of power and wealth better than most. Through both his parents there were family contacts with the dynasties of administrators and advisers who kept the powerful French monarchy operating (Febvre, 1969, pp. 145–61). His father was a royal financier who, following the death of his wife, had turned from high finance into high ecclesiastical office and become archbishop of Reims and a cardinal of the church. Unlike Briçonnet's uncle, the famous financier Semblançay, Briçonnet's father knew how important it was to make wealth respectable in sixteenth-century France. His son was the electoral agent for his father at the time of his elevation to Reims and became his vicar general. Thanks to his father, he was appointed bishop of

This cycle of events was clearly demonstrated in 1525–6. The humanist scholars and writers who enjoyed the king's protection were abruptly left defenceless by Francis I's capture at the battle of Pavia in February 1525. The queen mother and regent during his absence, Louise of Savoy, was no great patron to those of advanced opinions; in 1523 she had been sufficiently concerned about the growth of heresy to organize the dispatch of preachers to tour the most affected provinces during Advent. With the Peasants' War in Germany affecting Franche Comté and threatening to come further west, further damaging the unity of the realm in these critical months, neither she nor the judges were prepared to take any risks with heresy. They united in its persecution for the 12 months until the king's return from captivity in March 1526; with that the panic subsided and Francis criticized the Sorbonne for actively campaigning for orthodoxy in Paris and disturbing the peace. The special commission of judges to investigate heresy was replaced by an episcopal commission which included three theologians, two of whom were Erasmian in tendency. The reformers could breathe again. The same cycle was to repeat itself nine years later in 1534 with the infamous Day of Placards.

In any case, the authorities had often little conception of what the term 'Lutheran' actually meant. It was a broad brush with which to tar one's enemies, and, even on the eve of the civil wars 40 years later, French protestants would often still be referred to as 'Lutherans', more or less as a term of abuse. A long verse satire dated around 1530 called *The Lutherans' Hat* (*Le chappeau des Lutheriens*) already contained all the elements of popular and ill-informed anti-protestant sentiment which would be developed later on (Moore, 1930, ch. xi). You could be accused of being a Lutheran because you were a German-speaking student at a French university (there were a number of German 'nations' in French universities and they certainly helped to spread knowledge of Lutheranism in France). You risked being called a Lutheran for eating meat on a Friday or for stealing the Host (a surprisingly frequent occurrence in pre-reformation France, partly perhaps because the consecrated wafers used in the Mass were regarded as having magical powers). Hermits in the medieval eremetic tradition who had perhaps never heard

This cycle of events was clearly demonstrated in 1525–6. The humanist scholars and writers who enjoyed the king's protection were abruptly left defenceless by Francis I's capture at the battle of Pavia in February 1525. The queen mother and regent during his absence, Louise of Savoy, was no great patron to those of advanced opinions; in 1523 she had been sufficiently concerned about the growth of heresy to organize the dispatch of preachers to tour the most affected provinces during Advent. With the Peasants' War in Germany affecting Franche Comté and threatening to come further west, further damaging the unity of the realm in these critical months, neither she nor the judges were prepared to take any risks with heresy. They united in its persecution for the 12 months until the king's return from captivity in March 1526; with that the panic subsided and Francis criticized the Sorbonne for actively campaigning for orthodoxy in Paris and disturbing the peace. The special commission of judges to investigate heresy was replaced by an episcopal commission which included three theologians, two of whom were Erasmian in tendency. The reformers could breathe again. The same cycle was to repeat itself nine years later in 1534 with the infamous Day of Placards.

In any case, the authorities had often little conception of what the term 'Lutheran' actually meant. It was a broad brush with which to tar one's enemies, and, even on the eve of the civil wars 40 years later, French protestants would often still be referred to as 'Lutherans', more or less as a term of abuse. A long verse satire dated around 1530 called *The Lutherans' Hat* (*Le chappeau des Lutheriens*) already contained all the elements of popular and ill-informed anti-protestant sentiment which would be developed later on (Moore, 1930, ch. xi). You could be accused of being a Lutheran because you were a German-speaking student at a French university (there were a number of German 'nations' in French universities and they certainly helped to spread knowledge of Lutheranism in France). You risked being called a Lutheran for eating meat on a Friday or for stealing the Host (a surprisingly frequent occurrence in pre-reformation France, partly perhaps because the consecrated wafers used in the Mass were regarded as having magical powers). Hermits in the medieval eremetic tradition who had perhaps never heard of Luther risked being burned for heresy alongside Lutherans, as was the poor hermit of Livry outside Meaux in 1525. The Waldensians were called 'Lutherans' by the *parlement* of Provence in 1533 although they seem to have had little if any connection with the German reformer. When the Sorbonne sat down in 1544 to try to ban heretical works, it found itself issuing an index that was an extraordinary rag-bag of forbidden books, including works by Rabelais, Dolet, Erasmus, Lefèvre d'Etaples, as well as Luther, Calvin and Zwingli.

The position is complicated because those who were most attracted by what Luther or Zwingli wrote, avoided too overt a connection with other religious reformers outside France. Instead, they tended to stress their devotion to the gospel (*l'évangile*) of the true message of Jesus Christ, and, for the historian Imbart de La Tour, evangelism represented all those who wanted a reform along protestant lines but without wishing to establish a separate church in order to achieve it (1946, vol iii). We can best recreate some of the atmosphere of this group by looking at the language and themes of the early translations of Luther's writings in vernacular French, since these were the ones which most worried the authorities as likely to spread the word furthest.

At the latest count, there are 22 surviving printed editions known to bibliographers of the works of Luther translated into French before 1550 (Higman, 1984). Many were produced in the printing centres of the Rhineland in Basle and Strasburg and in Antwerp which had an established place in the French market; but a number of titles were also published by the remarkable Parisian printing house of Simon Dubois, which enjoyed the protection of the king's sister and moved to Angoulême in January 1529 to continue its activities without the harassment of the authorities in the capital (Berthoud, 1957, pp. 1–27). Generally speaking, they presented the principal doctrinal questions in Lutheranism, although they were anxious to avoid giving needless offence. The translation often altered the balance of the Lutheran original significantly in order to reduce controversy. They tended to be packaged in a relatively non-controversial way and to avoid becoming entangled in specific controversies about indulgences or the papacy. Their language was that of St Paul, faith, the Word, grace and sin, with an additional emphasis on idolatry and superstition, coupled with the vocabulary of redemption, sacrifice (of Christ), light (of the Gospels) and resurrection.

One of the earliest was Guillaume Farel's presentation of the Lord's Prayer and the Creed (the latter mainly a Lutheran translation), published in Basle in August 1524 (Higman, 1982). Farel (1489–1565) was one of those remarkably restless individuals who always happen to be in the right place at the right time. He grew up in the Dauphiné Alps (historians have often generously allowed him a Waldensian heritage), was trained in the university of Paris, moved to Meaux to be a companion of bishop Briçonnet, but then returned to Dauphiné before leaving France for a wandering life in the Rhineland. He then went on to form part of the French populations, at various times, of Strasburg, Basle, Metz, Montbéliard, Neuchâtel, Lausanne and, finally, Geneva, where he invited Calvin to join him in 1536. In an introduction to the book, Farel presented all the main themes of evangelism. The truth faith in Jesus Christ was being stifled by 'the great negligence of the shepherds'; 'God's flock have been badly instructed.' To stimulate a true faith, they needed the essential parts of Scripture simply expounded, particularly the Commandments and the Lord's Prayer. The work was for popular use by the 'congregation of the faithful'; it was not designed for 'a breakaway church'. But the exposition of the texts which followed was, of course, a clear statement of the Lutheran tenets of the preeminence of Scripture, of faith over works, and of the priesthood of all believers. It was reprinted the following year by a Parisian press which had close contacts in Basle under the title *The Prayer of Jesus Christ* (*l'Oraison de Jesuchrist*) (Higman, 1983, pp. 91–111). But this explicit presentation of the Lutheran message proved too rich to stomach in the wake of the events of 1525–6 and was watered down to become a part of the first edition of *The Book of True and Perfect Prayer* (*Livre de vraye et parfaicte oraison*), printed in 1528. On the title page was a famous woodcut, depicting Christ on the Mount of Olives with the disciples sleeping at his feet. This was to be the most popular book of evangelical piety in France, if we may measure this from the fact that it was reprinted no less than 14 times between 1528 and 1545. All the signs are that, despite the difficulties, dangers and slowness of translating and publishing reformed literature for the French market in the years before 1540, protestantism, in its looser and specifically French 'evangelical' context, had made considerable strides.

Briçonnet, Lefèvre d'Etaples and Marguerite of Navarre

In retrospect, it must have seemed to many French protestants that the days of 'magnificent religious anarchy' had been a mixed blessing; so many opportunities for evangelism had existed but the lack of a pre-eminent leader had left them powerless to exploit them. Theodore Beza (Théodore de Bèze, 1519–1605) reflected in his *Icones* of 1580 that 'France might have had another Luther in Louis de Berquin' and this was perhaps the case (Mann, 1934, p. 114); Berquin had the right qualifications in terms of education, background and friends. But the five years of conflict with the *parlement* and the Sorbonne in Paris gradually wore him down. The fact of the matter was that the heterodox conditions of the early French reform were not favourable to producing the kind of leadership which would be appropriate for the organized churches later on and so it was pointless to look for it. We may illustrate the point by examining the careers of three individuals at the emotional heart of the early French reformation; Guillaume Briçonnet, bishop of Meaux, the scholar Jacques Lefèvre d'Etaples, and the king's sister, Marguerite d'Angoulême.

Briçonnet (*c.*1472–1534) was the son of a family from the Loire valley which knew the corridors of power and wealth better than most. Through both his parents there were family contacts with the dynasties of administrators and advisers who kept the powerful French monarchy operating (Febvre, 1969, pp. 145–61). His father was a royal financier who, following the death of his wife, had turned from high finance into high ecclesiastical office and become archbishop of Reims and a cardinal of the church. Unlike Briçonnet's uncle, the famous financier Semblançay, Briçonnet's father knew how important it was to make wealth respectable in sixteenth-century France. His son was the electoral agent for his father at the time of his elevation to Reims and became his vicar general. Thanks to his father, he was appointed bishop of great letter-writer; the repertory of her surviving correspondence in 1930 listed 1,143 letters and, with new discoveries, this is now nearer 1,500 (Jourda, 1930; and Clive, 1983, pp. 55–6). She was also a creative writer of talent. Her meditative poem, *The Mirror of the Christian Soul*, first published in 1531, was highly popular and was reprinted in French seven times before the end of the decade. Other devotional works followed before the selection of her plays and poetry was published in the famous *Pearls from the Pearl of Princesses* (*Marguerites de la Marguerite des princesses*) in 1547. The *Heptaméron*, a light-weight sixteenth-century evangelical collection, only appeared after her death in 1559.

It is in her private correspondence, away from the complex and delicate questions of literary influence, that one can most easily appreciate her relationship to the early reform. For the period 1521–4, an intense exchange of letters between herself and bishop Briçonnet, the latter generally writing as her spiritual counsellor from 'her house' at Meaux, reveals one of the decisive influences on her religious and artistic development (Veissière, 1975–7). In richly allusive language, Briçonnet expounded to her some Dionysian and mystic ways to better spiritual awareness which would have been very familiar to Lefèvre and other members of the Meaux circle. Her later correspondence reveals how quietly determined she was to do all she could to protect and sustain the evangelical cause in France. Gérard Roussel became her confessor and almoner and, in 1536, was made bishop of the Navarre patrimonial diocese of Oloron. Lefèvre was given a quiet retirement in her court at Nérac. She employed Caroli as her preacher and curate on her estates at Alençon until he was forced to flee France in 1534. Wherever we see those of evangelical opinions surviving in France in the 1530s, it is to Marguerite of Navarre that we are tempted to look first to explain how and why. Her own religious views were not, of course, static, and she was to be open to both Lutheran and mature Calvinist opinions in her later life, but these were, as Febvre said, grafted on to the evangelism which she imbibed in the 1520s, and never distinct from it (Febvre, 1944, p. 144). Although a protector of evangelism, in so far as she had the power to be so, Marguerite refused to see it as a faction. As she said in her first poem, the *Dialogue in the Form of a Nocturnal Vision (Dialogue en forme de vision nocturne)*, written in 1524 but published nine years later:

> I beg you that these fractious debates
> About free will and liberty be left
> To the great scholars who, having [liberty], have it not:
> So pressed are their hearts by their inventions
> That Truth can no longer find its place ...
> Be assured that you are free indeed
> If you have the grace and love of God.

The common feature of these three important figures in the early French reformation was their consistent unwillingness to recognize or accept that the reformation was concerned with the making of a new religion and a new church and therefore a refusal to accept leadership and responsibility for any such development. The result was that, under an intensification of the repression of heresy, beginning around 1540, small groups of exiles from France in Strasburg, Basle, Neuchâtel and Geneva began to take matters into their own hands and organize the French reformation from without rather than from within.

2 Repression and the Growth of a Protestant Church

Those seeking a model of how to organize a reformed church in France in the 1530s and 1540s had only to turn to the German Rhineland, and particularly to Strasburg and Basle. When the evangelical community in Meaux sought to 'draw up' a church in 1546, it was to Strasburg and not Geneva that they sent their envoys to learn what they should do (*Histoire ecclésiastique*, 1883, vol i, p. 494). The importance of Strasburg to the French reformation was correctly divined by the catholic judge and friend of Montaigne, Florimond de Raemond, in 1605 (Raemond, 1605, pp. 837–8):

> Strasburg, they called it the New Jerusalem, enjoyed a close proximity to France. This was where the Hydra-Headed Heresy drew up its Arsenal and gathered together its various forces in order to come and assail us. Here was the retreat and rendezvous for Lutherans and Zwinglians under the leadership of Martin Bucer, the great enemy to catholics. This was the receptacle for those banished from France and the host to him who has given his name to calvinism. It was here that he constructed the Talmud of the new heresy, that instrument of our ruin. In short, this was where the first French church, as they call it, was drawn up to serve as a model and patron to those we have since seen everywhere in France.

Raemond was not exaggerating the influence of Strasburg on John Calvin or on the French reformation; and it is a regrettable but understandable consequence of a Genevan bias to the historical writing about the French reform that its role has often been obscured.

Strasburg was a large Rhineland town of about 20,000 inhabitants. It was an Imperial City (*Reichsstadt*) which meant that the emperor was its direct seigneur and it owed no allegiance to any independent authority in the Holy Roman Empire. It was also a free town (*freie Stadt*) and that meant that it owed its seigneur no obligations. Indeed, the city was not even obliged to take an oath of allegiance to the emperor. The old German proverb, 'the air of the city makes free' (*Die Stadtluft macht frei*), was never truer than in Strasburg. Its complicated municipal constitution was designed to ensure that no group ever secured a monopoly of power. In reality, though, power rested with an oligarchy of patrician families – the Sturm, the Wurmser, the Bock, etc. The reformation confronted them with a popular movement against the old ecclesiastical order, especially in the years 1523–5. Faced with iconoclastic riots and waves of anticlerical agitation, the city magistrates, unconstrained by any oath of allegiance to the emperor, plumped for the reformation. It was a brave move because they sacrificed a considerable amount for the social peace they hoped would result. Their family chapels and bequests to the cathedral disappeared along with the ecclesiastical patronage they had enjoyed, and there was no guarantee that the new church would be theirs to control. In addition, the diplomatic problems it posed for the city in the 1530s and 1540s were enough to turn the hair of any city magistrate white. The city took a gamble that it could put together a league of protestant princes, persuade the French king to put his influence behind it, and thus menace the emperor sufficiently to allow moderate protestant reform in the Reich to flourish. In the first, they succeeded at Schmalkalden in 1531; in the second, the largely failed, although it was not for want of trying in the mid-1530s and again in the mid–1540s. The result of that failure was to cost them dear. It allowed the emperor to threaten them with his troops in 1547, forcing the city to take a formal oath of allegiance to him, to accept the *Interim* of the empire and to re-establish catholic worship in the cathedral and two other churches of the city. After 1547, and even more so after the similarly menacing French invasion of Metz in 1552, the city was less welcoming towards French refugees who found it harder to gain the important status of *bourgeois*. In 1563, the magistrates closed the French church after over 30 years of existence, and Strasburg's distinctive role in the French reformation was largely at an end.

French exiles appeared in Strasburg as the first stages of its reformation were achieved in 1525, and their numbers were supplemented by renewed influxes in the two succeeding decades. They came not just from France but also from other French-speaking parts of Europe, such as the Walloon provinces of the southern Netherlands, Lorraine and the prince-bishopric of Liège. They formed a community apart and there was considerable intermarriage; John Calvin, for example, married Idelette de Bure, the daughter of an expatriate Liégeois there in 1540. But it would be wrong to imagine that this exiled community was a harmonious one, for, like most exiles, they felt frustrated and forgotten, and had time on their hands to devote to what were sometimes rather bitter doctrinal debates. Biblical exegesis, evangelization, episcopacy, the ministry, the doctrine of the Trinity and above all the sacrament of the Mass were all subjects of dispute, with the last proving the most divisive.

The view that the communion was a ritual of commemoration in which Christ's presence was in the hearts of men had already been cogently presented by the Swiss reformer Huldrych Zwingli, and it is not surprising to find his views quickly represented among the French exiles. Basle, the gateway to Switzerland, lies only 30 miles to the south of Strasburg, and it too had a refugee French protestant community, although it was not organized into a church before the 1550s. Basle joined the reform in February 1529 and, henceforth, Strasburg and Basle saw themselves as a community of Rhineland protestantism (a Christian Civic Union or *Christliche Burgrecht*). Their scholars and theologians were also close allies; Oecolampadius (John Hussgen, 1482–1531), the evangelist of Basle and supporter of Zwingli, was a friend and trusted colleague to the leader of the Strasburg reformation throughout this period, the French-speaking Martin Bucer (1491–1551). They were in agreement on the issue of the sacraments at the time of the important conference between Luther and Zwingli at Marburg in 1529. In the same year, they collaborated in organizing the new protestant ministry at Ulm, where they shared a conviction that the churches in these small urban republics needed greater independence from secular government and a more clearly defined set of functions in order to fulfil their preaching, educational and spiritual mission. When Oecolampadius died in 1531, Bucer wrote to a friend that 'we did not have a better theologian nor one more equipped to promote the creation [*instauratio*] of a church' (Livet et al., 1977, p. 338). In both respects Bucer was being over-generous to his friend's attainments but, between them, these two reformers were to have a tremendous importance in the French reform. Under their influence, it became 'sacramentarian' and learnt how to set up a separate church.

The Affair of Placards

The importance of the sacramentarian issue back in France became very clear in the famous Affair of Placards in the autumn of 1534. On Sunday morning, 18 October, Parisians on their way to Mass found protestant placards or broadsheets pasted up in several parts of the city. One of the originals has survived in Switzerland, and it does not at first sight look very dramatic. Somewhat smaller than the front cover of a modern tabloid newspaper, it consisted of a closely printed text in four paragraphs under the heading: 'True articles on the horrible, great and insufferable abuses of the papal mass' ('Articles véritables sur les horribles, grands & importables abuz de la Messe papalle') (Berthoud, 1957, pp. 119–20). Yet to Parisians, what it said and the manner in which it did so was truly revolutionary. For them – as for most of Christian Europe – the Mass was the regular and central event of social reconciliation, a vital ritual of pacification of enemies, both alive and dead. Here was a text which told them that the Mass was a priestly sham which 'seduced' the people, disinherited the human race and would destroy the world. The final savage paragraph of the placard ran:

> By this Mass they [the priests] have stabbed at, destroyed, snuffed out everything. They have disinherited kings, princes, merchants and everyone imaginable, both alive and dead. They can exist without resposibility to anyone, without duties, without the need

24

even to study ... Be not surprised then that they defend it with force. They kill, burn, destroy, and murder as brigands all those who contradict it; for, without force, they are defenceless. Truth menaces, compels, follows and chases them and it will find them out. By it shall they be destroyed. Fiat. Fiat. Amen.

The Mass was thus savaged and molested in a way which crudely distorted reformed theology. It could only have come from a French protestant in exile and we now know that it was the handiwork of Antoine Marcourt, an exile from Picardy who had become protestant minister in Neuchâtel in 1531. His talents as a publicist are well attested by his *Book of Merchants* (*Le Livre des marchands*, 1534), a bitter commentary on the financial aspects of church spirituality in the light of Christ's overturning of the money-changers' tables in the temple (Berthoud, 1973, ch. v).

The Parisian reaction was predictable (Knecht, 1982, pp. 248–52). A wave of sectarian hatred gripped the capital as it was rumoured that the reformers planned to sack the Louvre, burn down all the churches and murder the faithful at Mass. Foreigners came under suspicion and a Flemish merchant was lynched. The fear that this was but part of a wider conspiracy grew when it was learnt that similar placards had also been discovered in about 5 provincial towns and in the royal château at Blois. Within 24 hours, the *parlement* had taken the initiative to round up all possible protestant suspects and, by the end of November, 6 had already been burned. When the king returned to Paris, he set up a special commission of 12 magistrates to judge heresy cases, and a sub-commission to deal with potential suspects within the ranks of the judiciary itself. In an extraordinary general procession on 21 January 1535, Francis I joined the city corporations and the massed ranks of the royal relics (including the precious Crown of Thorns, rarely seen in public) behind a cortège in which the Blessed Sacrament, which the placards had outraged, was carried reverently beneath a canopy held by members of the royal house. After high mass at Notre-Dame, the king urged his subjects to denounce all heretics, even their close friends and relatives and the day ended with 6 more victims being burned at the stake. Many more followed before the wave of repression began to wane in June 1535. On 24 January a royal proclamation named 73 notable 'Lutherans' who were in hiding. The following week, an edict made those who sheltered heretics liable to the same fate as the heretics themselves and offered informers a quarter share of their victims' property.

It has recently been argued that the Affair of Placards was significant in transforming French protestantism in the minds of many contemporaries into a clearly defined 'religion for rebels' which had to be stamped out (Kelley, 1981, pp. 13–19). Certainly, it was much easier to identify – and thus to prosecute – those who refused to subscribe to the Mass. In addition, the placards were a direct attack on the priesthood and appeared to indicate a coordinated attempt at sedition at a time when the rising at Münster was making all Europe fearful of the social and political consequences of religious change. The affair thus both helped define orthodoxy and gave it new allies among the clergy and royal corporations whose task it was to preserve order. It also made it more difficult for those of heterodox opinion within France either to voice their opinions or enjoy protection in high places. Even Marguerite d'Angoulême faltered, having withdrawn from her brother's court to become queen regent of Navarre in Nérac; in 1542, she assured the king that nobody at her court was a 'sacramentarian' (Knecht, 1982, p. 390). Finally, it swelled the numbers of exiles abroad. The famous edict of Coucy of 16 July 1535, which brought the immediate wave of persecution to an end, offered many of them only the illusion of an amnesty and pardon. Sacramentarians were explicitly excluded from the pardon, and the amnesty only operated providing they abjured the Lutheran faith within six months of their return; recidivists thereafter were to be put to death without appeal (Sutherland, 1980, pp. 30 and 336).

But the extent to which the Placards mark a watershed should not be exaggerated, for the overall pattern of the 1530s was a cyclical one of repression followed by remission. It was also regional, and in many French provinces there was no perceptible change in repression in the years 1534–5. The definition of orthodoxy was not finally settled in France until 1543 when the confession of faith, drawn up by the Sorbonne, was accepted by the *parlements* and promulgated as a royal law (some catholics would argue later a 'fundamental' law).

Censorship could only be seen as coordinated and arranged on a national basis after the publication of the index of prohibited books by the Sorbonne in 1545. The various institutions charged with the enforcement of the decrees against heretics continued in disarray until a series of edicts in 1539–42 defined more clearly the competence of royal and ecclesiastical courts. Finally, the attitudes of Francis I cannot be said to have been irredeemably and substantially altered by the affair. One protestant in exile – John Calvin – thought the king might still be persuaded after 1535 to accept a measure of evangelical truth – at least this was the purpose of dedicating to him the famous treatise, the *Institution of the Christian Religion* (*Christianae religionis institutio*), in 1536.

John Calvin

John Calvin (1509–64) was among the least conspicuous of the French protestants to scuttle to safety in the wake of the Affair of Placards (Parker, 1975, chs i–iii). He was the son of a minor ecclesiastical official from the city of Noyon, 60 miles north-east of Paris, who had been educated at the university of Paris and had studied for a law degree at the university of Orléans. If he had any notoriety in 1535, it was as a precocious humanist who had published a commentary on Seneca's treatise *On Clemency* (*De Clementia*) in 1532. He drifted discreetly in evangelical affairs in 1533 and 1534, briefly coming into contact with the Parisian authorities in 1533 when an inaugural sermon by Nicolas Cop, rector of the university of Paris and his personal friend, revealed more evangelical sympathies than was prudent within the precincts of the faculty of theology. Calvin's rooms were searched and some letters confiscated, and he left the capital to stay with friends in Marguerite of Navarre's Angoulême before going on to her court at Nérac. In the wake of the Placards, his former Latin tutor and other friends were either arrested or fled into hiding and Calvin followed them. He eventually arrived in Basle in January 1535 and there in the company of a small group of French exiles, some former friends from the twilight world of French evangelism, he completed the first edition of the *Institution* that August, with publication following in March 1536.

No written work did more to determine the character of the French reformation than the *Institution*. It is, however, no easy matter to delineate how, for it was a subtle book, designed to fulfil several purposes at once, and these changed in the recensions and additions to the text which were made between 1536 and the final Latin edition of 1559. (These can be followed in the edition by J.T. McNeill, 1961.) The original was a small Latin book of some 500 pages, unevenly divided into 6 chapters. The full title (translated) is *The Institution of the Christian Religion, Containing almost the Whole sum of Piety and Whatever It is Necessary to Know in the Doctrine of Salvation*. Calvin's Latin is nothing if not alert to shades of meaning and he chose the words 'institution' (*institutio*), 'religion' (*religio*) and 'piety' (*pietas*) carefully. By 'institution' he meant not just the pillars and structures, as it were, of Christianity, but its instruction, education and indoctrination. This is why the first chapters were arranged round the topics of the Lutheran catechism already familiar to evangelist writers of the French reform: the Commandments, the Creed, the Lord's Prayer. 'Religion' was a word with comparative edge to it and was not in common currency in the first half of the sixteenth century, especially among those who preferred to believe that the Christendom of only one faith still existed. Calvin borrowed it from the pre-Christian classics to delineate the public profession of a true piety which would lead to salvation in a world largely bereft of it (and therefore damned). The title thus indicated the key tone of the pages which followed: measured but contentious advocacy of the 'religion' of the persecuted adherents of the French reform.

Within a year the first edition was out of print and Calvin set to work to produce a revised edition, which appeared in 1539, with 17 chapters, including new ones on important themes in Calvin's theology such as the knowledge of God and predestination and providence. A new preface spoke of the work as a 'textbook' to be used in 'the preparation of candidates in theology for the reading of the divine Word' and the folio edition allowed wider margins for student annotations. A French translation of this work, in which Calvin struggled to convey the nuances of meaning in the Latin text into the vernacular, appeared in Geneva in 1541, and it is some measure of the notoriety the book had already achieved in France that every effort was made to prevent its circulation there. The Sorbonne promptly outlawed it and in July 1542, and again in February 1544, stacks of copies were burned in front of Notre-Dame cathedral in Paris. Further Latin editions of 1543 and 1550 expanded the text still more culminating in the final Latin edition of 1559, a magnificent folio edition nearly 800 pages long which, as the title indicated, had been completely re-arranged to form almost a new book. This is the version which would leave its lasting mark on the French reformed church and the one which would find its way on to the shelves of French protestants who could afford it. Containing a system of doctrine and its history, a creed, a theology, a manual of ethics, an ecclesiology and a guide to controversy, it was now the very full handbook of a separate religion.

Geneva and the French Reform

The *Institution* made it clear that, when it comes to establishing a church, there was a critical distinction, between a community of believers (what was known as an *église plantée*) and what was termed a 'gathered' church (*église dressée*). The latter needed a preaching ministry dispensing sacraments, a liturgy, a pattern of worship, a catechism and a discipline. Calvin's experiment in establishing a church took place in Geneva where he became permanently resident from September 1541. But this was only after a turbulent six-year period which had involved him in an unsuccessful attempt to impose a reformed discipline in Geneva between August 1536 and April 1538, followed by refuge in Basle and Strasburg.

Calvin learnt all he needed to know about establishing a church from his period in Strasburg (Livet et al., 1977, pp. 285–91). His first liturgy was written in 1539 for the French refugees there and included a translation of Martin Bucer's stark confession, which Calvin used on his death-bed and which Beza recited before the colloquy of Poissy in 1561. He published a less rigorous version for use in Geneva in 1542. A liturgy implied a hymnology and this too was begun under Strasburg influence. Calvin put some psalms into verse in 1538, beginning with Psalm 46 which was already available in the famous Lutheran version ('Our God is Our Firm

Support' – *Nostre Dieu nous est ferme appui*). In 1539, he utilized 16 of the verse settings of the Psalms presented to Francis I by the poet Clément Marot, and also arranged the Creed and the Commandments for musical accompaniment (*Aucuns pseaulmes et cantiques mys en chant*, published in facsimile by D. Delétra in 1919). The melodies were supplied by two Strasburg musicians, Matheis Greiter and Wolfgang Dachstein, and this was the authentic origin of the famous Huguenot Psalter. Greiter wrote the haunting lyric to Psalm 68, ('Let God arise, let his enemies be scattered'), the 'battle hymn' of the Huguenots on the eve of the first civil war. Calvin's second catechism, published in Geneva in 1542 and composed of 373 questions and answers, was inspired by Martin Bucer's and was entirely different in form from the first which had been published in Geneva in 1537. The rigorous sub-division of ministerial responsibility into four orders (pastors, deacons, elders and teachers) formed the basis of the famous *Ecclesiastical Ordinances*, or constitution, of the Genevan church submitted by Calvin to the Genevan magistrates in November 1541, and was directly borrowed from Bucer's *Commentaries* on the Epistle to the Romans and the Gospels, both published in 1536. For ecclesiastical discipline, Calvin was also indebted to Bucer and Strasbourg practice. In 1531, Bucer had succeeded in establishing (following Oecolampadius in Basle) a regime of 21 church ancients or elders (*Kirchenpfleger*), corresponding to the divisions of the city, who would act as the key constituent elements of ecclesiastical discipline. In 1534, this was reinforced by an acceptance in Strasburg of the power of excommunication resting with the church. Both would become essential elements of Calvin's Genevan ordinances (Wendel, 1942, pp. 179–97). To support the work of the teachers, Calvin also proposed the establishment of a college or high school and it is clear that he had been deeply influenced at Strasburg by the opening of John Sturm's high school, in which Bucer had taken a personal and detailed interest.

Geneva was, however, a very different city from Strasburg, It was half its size and nowhere near so wealthy or cosmopolitan. The reformation had come late to a city already bitterly divided between supporters of its powerful near neighbours, the canton of Berne and the duchy of Savoy (Monter,

1967). For over ten years after his arrival in 1541, Calvin had to contend with a politically powerful internal opposition. It weakened gradually under the relentless and remarkable preaching and teaching efforts of Calvin and the other protestant ministers who joined him there. Their efforts were assisted by the changing composition of the city's population as a result of the arrival of refugees from France and Italy.

Geneva was on France's door-step, the more so since the duchy of Savoy, which enveloped Geneva on almost three sides, had been annexed by the king of France in 1536 and would remain so until 1559. It is therefore not surprising to find French protestant refugees beginning to arrive in significant numbers towards the end of the 1540s. In 1549, the city council began to keep a register of those refugees arriving in the city along the routes from Lyon, Burgundy and Turin who applied for the status of *habitant*. The record is by no means complete, but it totalled almost 5,000 names before the register ceased in January 1560. Unfortunately, under-registration is clear and other sources suggest that the real figure is closer to 10,000, with more in the latter half of the decade than in the earlier (Monter, 1979, pp. 402–12). This was an enormous influx which, whilst it did not immediately change the political composition of the city (*habitants* did not have the political rights of the *bourgeois*), altered its economy in ways which no city magistrate could ignore. Bursaries and charity had to be organized for them, as well as housing and accommodation. One reason for the opening of the college in 1558, followed by the academy in the following year, was to provide an academic foundation for those refugees who wanted to enter the ministry. By 1560, the congregation of Genevan ministers was heavily committed – although the city magistrates studiously denied it to the French authorities – to the final training and dispatch of ministers in response to pressing demands for them from communities in France (Kingdon, 1956, especially ch vi).

The changing face of the city is perhaps most evident in the case of the printing industry. Between 1530 and 1540 only 42 titles had been printed in the city (Febvre and Martin, 1976, p. 315). Between 1540 and 1550, there were 193 editions published, and this rose to over 500 in the period between 1550 and 1564. By then, about 40 presses were

31

working, largely employing the printers and booksellers exiled from France – between 1550 and 1560, more than 130 had arrived. Protestant literature for the French market became a substantial business, controlled by a small group of emigré entrepreneurs such as Jean Crespin, Antoine Vincent and Laurent de Normandie. Never would the ethos of Calvinism and capitalism be more closely allied!

Geneva's insignificance before 1550 was gradually replaced by a growing authority and influence over the French reformation in the decade of the 1550s. The edict of Compiègne (24 July 1557) tried to stop the flow of exiles to the city, as well as the passage of forbidden literature out of it; two years later, in the peace of Câteau-Cambrésis, Henry II of France and Philip II of Spain agreed to work together to eliminate Genevan heresy. Three years later, the edict of Amboise (March 1560) tried to stop missionary pastors entering France from Genevan territory. Geneva's rapidly growing importance was never underestimated by the authorities who did their best to prevent the growth of heresy.

The Legal Repression of Heresy

The explanation for the increased numbers of exiles in Geneva in the 1540s and 1550s lies, of course, in the nature of the legal repression of heresy in France in these years and, in order to understand that, we should imagine a typical suspect inside the prisons and courtrooms of sixteenth-century France. Nearly all heresy cases began with a denunciation, for heretics could rarely be caught 'red-handed'. In this, as in other respects, they were identical to witchcraft trials. The denunciation frequently came from clergymen, from inquisitors and also from convicted heretics; one suspect often led to several. Denunciation was a capricious business. The denouncer was not, strictly speaking, a party in the case. He stood to lose nothing, was obliged to undertake no sworn testimony, faced no costs, yet he held the accused under a strong presumption of guilt until his innocence was demonstrated and, from 1535 onwards, could expect to be rewarded from the possessions of the guilty. It is hardly surprising that heresy trials could serve ambition and revenge as much as religious purity. The only safeguard lay in the threat of countersuit from the accused for false defamation, but this course lay open only to those of some standing and financial means. Denouncing the wealthy, or those in authority and with powerful protectors, was therefore a risky business and best avoided. The actual trial began with the enquiry or inquisition from which the medieval institution gained its name. This generally consisted of depositions against the accused made under oath of secrecy and collected by the judges. Testimony from the socially and religiously prominent carried weight and, if favourable to the accused, might bring proceedings to a halt. The resistance of rural communities to interference from the outside could also ensure that the dossier remained a slight one. Conversely, where we find heresy proceedings in full swing in rural France, we may take it as some evidence of the breakdown, for whatever reason, of village and communal solidarities. Often the testimony was inconclusive or difficult to assess. Was a parish priest who contended that burial in a neighbouring and predatory Franciscan monastery would deny a dead person entry to purgatory a heretic? Was failure to pay tithe (quite common, as one might expect, in sixteenth-century France) a heresy? Did the accusation that an individual was trying to fabricate gold by magical means imply heresy rather than felony (the two crimes were often hard to disentangle)?

The dossier against a prior in Toulouse in 1546 may be taken as typical of the problems facing judges. He was reported as saying in the course of an argument in a master cutler's house there that he thought there was only one invisible church, located in the heavens and the hearts of men. His opponents said that they produced a copy of the 1543 articles of faith of the faculty of theology to confound him, but he had refused to accept that the king had sanctioned such rubbish; instead he had made a pass at the cutler's wife, slapped her on the buttocks and invited her to come with him to hear the Lenten sermon at the popular city church of the Daurade. But how much could they trust this denunciation? What had the prior meant? Had the case involved public disorder?

What happened next depended upon answers to these questions. It was also important whether you were a clergyman or a layman. The jurisdictional problems involved in heresy trials were clarified in three royal edicts of Paris (24 June

1539), Fontainebleau (1 June 1540) and Paris (23 July 1543) (Sutherland, 1980, pp. 33–5 and 337–40). Henceforth, ecclesiastical courts were to be restricted to the proof of heresy in clergymen and what were known as common crimes of heresy among the laity (*délits communs*). All other cases were reserved (*cas privilégiés*) for the royal courts, the senechalcies and the criminal chambers of the *parlements*. The distinction made here between a common crime of heresy and reserved cases, which justified the almost complete annexing of heresy cases to the royal courts, was based on whether the heresy had involved any degree of public scandal, offence, popular unrest or (in some edicts) sedition. In practice, almost every case could be 'evoked' by the royal prosecutor from ecclesiastical jurisdiction on these grounds. After 1542, cases of heresy were barely concerned with determining the orthodoxy of what people believed but with judging in a much more rough and ready way how people had behaved. From 1542 onwards, the definition of heresy broadened and deepened. It could include schoolmasters who interpreted the Scriptures (1539), iconoclasm (1551), secret meetings of all kinds (1551), the sale and distribution of heretic books (many edicts), and those who spoke 'words contrary to the Holy Catholic faith and the Christian religion'; for the first time, speaking became a felony. The edicts of Châteaubriant (27 June 1551) and Compiègne (24 July 1557) both included clauses against individuals who were associated with Geneva, forbidding subjects to correspond with, send money to, or otherwise favour those who left the kingdom to reside there. Bearers of letters and books from Geneva were subject to automatic arrest as 'heretics and disturbers of public peace and tranquillity'. The act of having been there became punishable by death (Sutherland, 1980, pp. 342–3; 344–5).

If there was a case to answer in the royal courts, the suspect was summoned to appear within three days ('trois briefs jours'). Unless immediately arrested, common sense dictated to most suspects that they disappear, and, even for those arrested on trial, escape from sixteenth-century prisons was relatively simple. Many of those who thus appeared in Geneva were not, strictly speaking, refugees, but fugitives from justice. The interrogation of those arrested proceeded according to established rules, but the accused had no recourse to legal counsel and were denied access to the evidence collected against them. In the course of interrogation, some confessions of guilt were extracted but it was customary, given the processes of Roman law on which French royal law in this area was based, to have recourse to torture. Again, there were rules for its use and these included the rule that the suspect had to sustain his confession for a day or so after the ordeal and that it could only be applied once, unless substantial new information had been added to the dossier. The frequency of torture for heresy was apparently much less than for other serious crimes such as homicide, forgery and infanticide, presumably, at least in part, because greater opportunity existed for individual testimony against the accused in heresy cases than in others.

The punishments for heresy were an odd assortment, ranging from the relatively innocuous public censure (*amende honorable*) and fine to the more draconian confiscation of goods and property, fustigation, banishment to the galleys and death by burning. Capital punishments were confirmed by the *parlements* before being carried out, until the edict of Châteaubriant (27 June 1551) permitted lesser courts (the *présidiaux* were established in the following year) to proceed against heretics without appeal to the sovereign courts. The lawyer in Calvin was appalled at this 'frightful' law, commenting acidly that Christians were thus denied the rights of appeal open to convicted forgers and thieves (Potter and Greengrass, 1983, p. 145). The courts had no desire to confer a martyr's crown and there is some evidence that the *parlements* took care to make the punishment match the crime. This is apparent in the case of an individual who styled himself John the Evangelist (Jehan l'Evangéliste), who was arrested in the early summer of 1553 by the *parlement* of Bordeaux for preaching in the Garonne valley (Mentzer, 1984, p. 118). The *parlement* ordered his great beard to be clipped and his long hair to be cut off before expelling him from the region. He wandered off and was next found preaching near Toulouse, where he was arrested and ordered to be confined in the Dominican monastery there. Unfortunately John's evangelism was compulsive and, in view of his 'rash, execrable and scandalous' utterances, the *parlement* decided to put him in solitary confinement in a small cell at the top of the tower of their prison. Only a year later, after he had set fire to his cell and nearly the whole of the prison, was he commanded to have his tongue cut out and then be led to the stake and burnt.

These burnings were exemplary sentences at the heart of public ceremonies designed to purify a community and present openly the dangers of heresy. Our knowledge of them is forever shaped by the French protestant martyrology, the *Book of Martyrs* (*Livre des martyrs*), compiled and published by the remarkable refugee printer in Geneva, Jean Crespin. It first appeared in 1554 as a slim volume and was continually added to in subsequent editions until 1609 (Gilmont, 1981). By making its readers aware of the courage of those who had suffered for their faith, Crespin's work was undeniably important in helping French protestant morale during the civil wars. It also enabled Calvinists to lay claim to the pure traditions of the early Christian church, which had also suffered from persecution at its birth. But its detail and overall impression may be misleading. First, it is not clear whether Crespin relates the constancy of, and public sympathy for, these victims accurately. He reports, for example, that one François d'Augi was burned for heresy in 1545 by the *parlement* of Toulouse and that, at the moment of execution, d'Augi 'was heard to cry out in a loud voice amidst the flames: "Courage, my brothers; I see the opened heavens and the Son of God who prepares to receive me".' But the archives of the *parlement* date his execution to 31 July 1551 and record that he was to be strangled before burning (Mentzer, 1984, p. 121). Second, those burnt were a very small proportion of the total number of suspects investigated. Of the 1,074 known heresy suspects appearing before the *parlement* of Toulouse, which had a fearsome reputation for cruelty among French protestants, only 62 (less than 6 per cent) died at the stake. In Paris the so-called 'Burning Chamber' (*Chambre ardente*), established by the king between May 1547 and March 1550 exclusively to handle cases of heresy, investigated 557 suspects, but ordered only 39 to be burnt (7 per cent). The *parlement* of Bordeaux, whose archives are less complete and which had a smaller area of jurisdiction, pursued 477 suspects between 1541 and 1559 of whom only 18 (less than 4 per cent) perished by fire (Mentzer, 1984, p. 101).

We shall never know precisely how many heresy suspects

were investigated in France before the civil wars. There were 9 sovereign courts (*parlements*) in 1559, but the disappearance of some records and the daunting bulk of others make any precise estimate almost impossible. It would not have been fewer than 5,000 and might have been as many as 8,000. The gathering pace of investigation is clearly presented in the available figures from the reasonably complete records of the *parlement* of Toulouse, and the following list details the numbers of accused heretics per decade there:

1511–20	4
1521–30	8
1531–40	121
1541–50	257
1551–60	684

This ascending curve of investigation and prosecution reflects as much the climate of fear produced by changes in statutes and methods of prosecution, as the growth of heresy; for it was in the nature of things that, as with witchcraft, the more you looked for it, the more you found.

Everything that we know about the sixteenth-century legal system suggests its manifest inability to enforce its authority uniformly and effectively and we should not expect it to have performed markedly better in the pursuit of heresy than of other crimes. Francis I and Henry II's chancellors came up with a variety of devices to try and make the system work better. *Parlements* were suspended and replaced by Parisian judges on commission (as in Normandy and Provence). Judges on assize (*grands jours*) were dispatched to regions which were remote from the arm of the sovereign law courts, such as Nîmes in 1541, or Béziers in 1550. They were also preoccupied with the possibility of heresy among the judges themselves, not an unreasonable fear, given the widespread hereditability of offices. By the edict of Châteaubriant (27 June 1551), all royal judges were required to take an oath of catholic allegiance before a *parlement*. Later, in 1557, Henry II proposed the establishment of a proper inquisition under three cardinals to reduce the possibility of heretical contamination among his judges blunting the effectiveness of his decrees; but he failed to convince the judges and the proposal was doomed. Some *parlements*, such as that in Dauphiné, remained renowned for their internal divisions and leniency towards protestant heretics. Others, like that in neighbouring Provence, gained an unenviable reputation for their vindictiveness towards the Waldensians of Mérindol and Cabrières whose communities were wiped out in the repression of 1543 (Knecht, 1982, pp. 401–2). Everywhere they had difficulty enforcing royal decrees in the more distant parts of their jurisdictions. Pockets of immunity would therefore continue to exist for protestantism almost everywhere within France, but particularly in the big cities and on the domains of the powerful nobility who protected their tenantry from judicial enquiry; and it is in these enclaves that the Calvinist churches of France were to congregate.

The Establishment of Calvinist Churches

Under the shadow of repression, protestant communities gradually coalesced in the 1550s. How they did so, and what their relationships were with Geneva, are questions not easily answered, for their activities were clandestine. Meetings often took place at night and with unavoidable secrecy. Missionaries from Geneva regularly used pseudonyms to disguise their identity and activity. We can glimpse the way things may have happened generally by looking at the growth of the Calvinist church in and around Poitiers, the 'mother congregation' of the French reformed church (Kingdon, 1956, p. 2).

Poitiers was a small university town, within the jurisdiction of the Paris *parlement* but almost as far from the influence of its judges as it was possible to be. Calvin had almost certainly spent some time there in or around June 1534, and he liked to think that he had helped to lay the roots for a reformed congregation there. Certainly a cluster of developing protestant communities existed in the surrounding region by the late 1540s, for 56 individuals were subsequently cited from Poitou before the 'Burning Chamber' (Dez, 1936, p. 18). Whether the congregation in Poitiers really met in the caves close to the town, like the early Christians in Rome, depends on one's respect for a local oral tradition. What does seem to be true, however, is that Geneva played little or no part in the process before 1554.

Calvin's curious neglect of the French congregations before this date is a matter for speculation. He certainly regarded obedience to established authority as sacred and would have had grave reservations about encouraging anything which looked subversive. Perhaps he still expected something of the French king Henry II who was, after all, the first French monarch not to swear specifically in his coronation oath to fight heresy in his dominions. Henry seemed committed to the reform of the French catholic church and, on 18 February 1551, had addressed a letter to every bishop of the realm, blaming the priesthood for the 'enormous faults, errors, abuses and scandals flourishing in Christianity' and requiring each bishop to organize a full diocesan visitation immediately. This was but one part of a conflict with the new pope, Julius III, who had recalled the council of Trent and who seemed to be turning into an imperial puppet. At the French court some of Henry's advisers believed that the key to French foreign policy lay in a firm alliance with the protestant princes of north Germany, who held the key to imperial communications with the Low Countries, possessed the most important reservoir of troops on which France might rely, and could keep the Holy Roman Empire weak and divided (Pariset, 1981). Calvin may have hoped, particularly in 1551–2, that the French king might be persuaded to moderate his repression, even to create a Gallican, reformed church.

By 1554, all this had proved an illusion, and in a letter, probably to the faithful of Poitiers, we find Calvin now giving advice on how to 'gather' a church (Potter and Greengrass, 1983, p. 152). They should not, he advised, try to rush things. To meet quietly in secret for the benefit of mutual support, reading the Gospel, singing psalms and hearing the Word was commendable and what a community of the faithful should do, even in the face of hostile repression. But to try to establish a church without the 'firm foundations' of a discipline in which they could elect a minister, 'chosen by you all in common', distribute the sacraments and baptize children without fear of 'contamination' from papal superstition, would be to separate themselves from the true faith of Jesus Christ. He must have been impressed with their

39

determination, though, for the first 'missionary' pastor to be sent by the company of pastors from Geneva into France, a student called Jacques l'Anglois, was dispatched the following year to the church in Poitiers.

Things were not easy for the Poitiers church. It soon became bitterly divided between supporters of l'Anglois and those of a Poitevin who openly supported the tolerant notions of Calvin's adversary in exile at Basle, Castellio. Later, l'Anglois caused another storm when he arrived in the new church at Tours uninvited by the congregation at large and challenged the authority of a newly appointed minister. The company of pastors in Geneva was invited to mediate in the embarrassing dispute, but it cautiously told the faithful in Tours that it could not interfere. Meanwhile Calvin had to write to another French church that it was on no account to consider armed resistance to established authority, no matter how fierce the repression. In all, only 88 ministers are recorded as having been sent out from the company of pastors in Geneva in the period from 1555 to 1562. This was a very small number, clearly inadequate for the number of congregations there must have been in France by the end of the decade. When the first measure of toleration permitted these groups of the faithful to come into the open, the Genevan company of pastors was deluged with requests for ministers which it was powerless to satisfy. People wanted ministers, Calvin wrote in 1561, 'with a desire as great as the sacraments are coveted among papists'. All the signs are, in fact, that the birth of the Calvinist church in France was a rather messy affair which Geneva was not in a position to control or direct.

This helps to explain the pressures for the elaboration of a formal 'discipline' in the French church. The first of which we are aware was produced, predictably, by the church in Poitiers. Headed the 'Political Articles for the reformed church of the Holy Gospel, drawn up in Poitiers, 1557', this primitive constitution for the French churches decreed a discipline regulating the selection of ministers, deacons and elders as well as membership of the churches and the control of morals. Nothing suggests that Calvin or Geneva had a direct part in it and it left many constitutional questions unanswered. These confusions became more conspicuous at the more important meeting of such representatives of the French churches as could get to Paris in 1559 – a meeting generally accepted to be the first national synod. The delegates endorsed two documents, a 'Confession of Faith' and a 'Discipline'. In both there was an element of contradiction about whether the churches were really under a common discipline and whether ultimate authority in them lay with their consistories and officers, or with their congregations as a whole (Lloyd, 1983, pp. 128–30). The delegates were trying to legitimize their own authority and the actions of the recent past and, at the same time, provide a clear national constitution for the reformed church in France. In the years between 1557 and 1562 it may well have been the sense of gathering numbers and imminent victory coupled with the organizing power of the Calvinist nobility that created a national French church, rather than either Genevan initiative or the uniting force of a Calvinist church constitution.

3 The Social Geography of French Protestantism

What sorts of people, and what kinds of places, were most attracted towards protestantism in sixteenth-century France? The answers to these questions are neither straightforward nor conclusive, not least because individuals in France exercised nothing approaching free religious choice. Even in the 'wonder-years' of 1561–2 when the protestants would enjoy 'elbow-room' greater than at any other time in the century, the new religion was still constrained by semi-official intolerance and popular sectarian hatred. The social geography of French protestantism thus reflects the repression of its formative years. It was also moulded by the social environment which varied from locality to locality. France was by far the most populous country in sixteenth-century Europe with a population which may have approached 20 million; it was also remarkably diverse, with provinces and regions (*pays*) enjoying their own institutions and languages. French protestantism could not fail to reflect this regionalism. It is also self-evident but important to observe that the spread of protestantism followed the social and geographic contours of catholic loyalties in France; we are concentrating here on one side only of a two-part equation.

How Many French Protestants?

How many protestants were there in France in the sixteenth century? The question is impossible to answer, since all but a handful of the relevant birth registers for protestant communities have disappeared. The best that we can do is to use the estimated numbers of 'gathered' churches. In March 1562, admiral de Coligny is supposed to have ordered the preparation of a list of the 2,150 churches then extant in France, to present to the regent Catherine de Médicis. Historians who have accepted this figure have neglected to notice that instructions were also issued that 'the more churches that can be included, the better' in order to frighten and impress the queen regent (Meylan and Dufour, 1976–, vol. iii, pp. 280–1). Subsequent efforts by the French pastor and historian Samuel Mours to collate evidence of every protestant community which appeared to exist in the second half of the sixteenth century could only reach a figure of 1,700 by including the independent principality of Béarn and numerous communities which, in reality, were unlikely ever to have had their own pastor and which existed only as an 'annexe' to another, larger church. We should therefore imagine that France (excluding Béarn and keeping to the frontiers established in 1559) had no more than between 1,200 and 1,250 churches in the decade 1560–70 or less than 4 per cent of the Catholic parishes of the kingdom (Garrisson-Estèbe, 1980, pp. 64–7). By the reign of Henri iv, 40 years later, new estimates were produced by the national synods of 1598, 1601 and 1607. They varied quite widely and none of them should be taken as precise calculations, but they all presented the number of churches as having declined by well over 50 per cent. Similar estimates a generation later from the national synod of 1637 suggest a further considerable contraction in the course of the first third of the seventeenth century. French protestantism had, in fact, reached its zenith in the first decade of the civil wars. We know some of the churches were very large: Rouen, for example, had an estimated congregation of 16,500 in 1565 (Benedict, 1981, p. 53). If we allow generously for 1,500 communicating members of each church, we arrive at an adult protestant population of under 2 million but perhaps approaching 10 per cent of the total population.

The churches were unevenly distributed throughout the French provinces. The accompanying map reveals the disparity, evident at an early stage and only reinforced by the events of the civil wars, between the protestant presence in northern France (roughly defined as those provinces north of the Loire) and the now familiar 'Huguenot crescent' of numerous congregations stretching in a broad arc across southern France

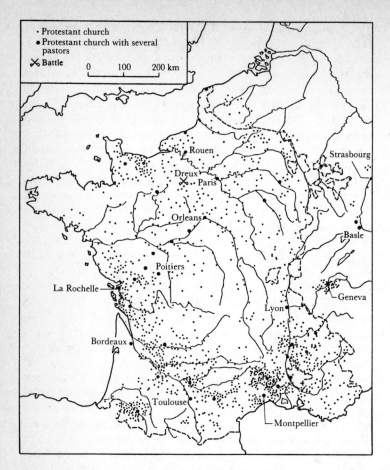

Map 1   French protestantism in 1562 (Mandrou, 1975)

from La Rochelle to the Dauphiné valleys. Also of importance are the areas where protestantism failed to make any appreciable showing. There are, for example, the 'frontier' zones of Picardy, Champagne and Burgundy (where catholicism and national identity seem to have coalesced and inoculated the provincial gentry against protestantism), and the Pyrenees (where the need to preserve links with catholic Spain was of importance), or the more interesting case of Brittany and the

Vendée in whose dioceses it is possible to hypothesize, as perplexed catholic priests and missionaries did towards the end of the century, that Christianity was as new to many of their inhabitants as it was to the savages of the New World (Croix, 1981, vol ii, pp. 1179–83; Delumeau, 1977, pp. 161–2).

There is no entirely plausible overall explanation for the concentration of churches in the Midi. Genevan influence is insufficient to explain it; almost as many inhabitants from the province of Normandy obtained the status of *habitant* there in the period 1549–60 as did those from the larger province of Languedoc (Mandrou, 1975, pp. 81–2; cf. Geisendorf, 1963, pp. 239–49). The existence of protestant 'refuges' closer to hand in the principalities of Orange or Béarn was probably more important; but then, similar points of refuge also existed for northern France in the Channel Islands, London, Sedan or, after 1572, the northern Netherlands. Protestantism certainly did not 'follow the book'; rather the reverse, since book production and distribution were concentrated heavily in northern France (Garrisson-Estèbe, 1980, pp. 37–9; also Martin and Chartier, 1982, pp. 351–63). Literacy was, of course, of considerable importance to the growth of protestantism but there is no evidence in the first usable surveys in the early nineteenth century that the south of France was generally more literate than the north, although there is a suggestion that those rural areas which had seen a strong protestant presence enjoyed higher literacy rates. This may, however, measure an effect rather than a cause (Chartier, Compère and Julia, 1976, pp. 17; 23–6). It would be convenient to relate the appeal of French protestantism to regional identity, but unfortunately the evidence points both ways. On the one hand, protestantism was linguistically French-dominated and appealed to those parts of southern French society which were most proud of their French linguistic affiliations; almost no effort was made to translate and publish the protestant scriptures or liturgy into dialects and we have no evidence of widespread use of *patois* in preaching. On the other hand, it is clear that it served the purposes of some of the notables in southern provinces, particularly in Languedoc or Béarn, to graft the protestant movement on to their governing institutions and to identify its survival with theirs. To the extent that the south of France had more active and powerful *pays*, this was, of course, important. More hesitantly, some protestant ministers sought to identify their cause with that of the older medieval provincial heresy of the Cathars but they did not push the comparison very far; they knew what had happened to the Cathars. The Calvinist crescent is probably only explicable as an amalgam of such things as the consequences of noble patronage, its small towns with their proud elites of notaries, schoolmasters, city worthies and strong artisanal networks reaching out into the countryside, and the relatively light weight of the royal official presence.

The Social Environment of French Protestantism

Contemporary comment as to which groups supported the protestant movement on the eve of the civil wars is almost invariably coloured by ignorance or prejudice. It is no surprise, for instance, to find the catholic soldier and royal lieutenant in Gascony, Blaise de Monluc, complaining in his memoirs that 'the majority of those who are mixed up in the (royal) finances are of this religion … and, worse, that the judges of the *parlements*, senechalcies and elsewhere abandon the old religion and the king and take to the new' (Garrisson-Estèbe, 1980, p. 15). He had a visceral hatred of the pedantry of the *robe* and a touching belief that there was little that the short, sharp shock of a military campaign could not solve. Florimond de Raemond, one of that group of judges in Bordeaux which Monluc despised, wrote: 'Those who first heard the "truth" (for this was their password) were goldsmiths, masons, carpenters and other miserable wage-earners, even down to those who had managed nothing other than a plough or a spade and who, overnight, became first-class theologians (p. 15). Here was a recently ennobled royal official's contempt for the third estate. Jean Michieli, Venetian ambassador in 1561, reported that it was 'the nobles who were above all contaminated, and particularly those under forty years of age' (p. 15); sweet revenge written for Italian eyes after the years of French military intervention in the peninsula during the Habsburg-Valois wars! Each had different impressions but they all agreed that French protestantism was gaining ground daily, on the eve of the civil wars.

To present a more objective picture, historians have tried to quantify the social appeal of French protestantism, using three sorts of documentation: the registers of royal courts recording heresy cases before 1559; the evidence from the status of refugees arriving in Geneva; and proscription lists of suspected Huguenots drawn up in catholic towns and cities in the civil wars (see appendix). Each source has its inevitable limitations. Not all heresy suspects before 1559 were protestants and, as we have already noted, certain groups tended not to appear before the courts while others may have been pursued with greater severity. This has to be remembered when analysing the statistics from the *parlements* of Paris and Toulouse. The number of exiles in Geneva who applied for the status of inhabitant naturally over-represents the mobile elements in the social fabric of French protestantism. The social composition of the exiles in Geneva changed quite dramatically in the course of the period 1549–60; the decade began with the refuge of the predominantly well-to-do and ended with the exile of the artisans and journeymen but it is unlikely that this change represented an equivalent shift in the overall social appeal of protestantism in France. The lists drawn up of those of 'ill-will towards the catholic faith' ('*malsentant envers la foi catholique*) survive from a variety of urban environments; Montpellier, Toulouse and Grenoble have been chosen because the samples are large. They are useful but rarely mention women or young people whom other sources cite as important constituent elements of urban protestantism; moreover the politics of proscription often ensured that prominent individuals found themselves suspected on somewhat flimsy pretexts. They were, in short, part of a rough and ready catholic reprisal. Inevitably, therefore, these are inappropriate sources with which to measure either noble or rural protestantism.

Protestantism among the Nobility and Clergy

French society was, formally speaking, dominated by the privileged orders of the first and second (clerical and noble) estates. To what extent did protestantism penetrate their

47

ranks? The judicial records present most clearly the support for the protestant reformation from the clergy. The first socially identifiable protestants tended to be clerics. This 'clerical treason' is most obvious among the lower clergy and the regular orders. It should occasion little surprise, given the material circumstances in the traditional church to which we have already alluded. In addition, there is now a growing body of evidence to suggest that the revenues of the church in the forms of bequests for commemorative prayers (*obits*) and masses for the dead (*neuvaines, trentaines* and *anniversaires* or *caps d'an*) were declining in many regions of France in the 1540s and 1550s, though not necessarily as a result of heretical influence (Nicholls, 1981, pp. 185–97; Molinier, 1984, pp. 240–60). This undoubtedly contributed to the climate in which heresy could survive, not least among a clergy whose income was thus threatened. Among the regular orders, the Augustinians, traditionally at odds with their Dominican rivals, were particularly prominent. In 1549, for example, 32 novices deserted the Augustinian friary in Rouen for protestantism, creating a public scandal (Nicholls, 1980, p. 279). Screened for doctrinal purity and retrained, a minority of clerical apostates was permitted to join the Calvinist missionary ministers in France on the eve of the civil wars (Kingdon, 1956, p. 4).

The higher clergy was not immune but it was only in April 1563 that the papacy summoned up its courage and undertook the unusual and difficult task of citing eight French bishops before the Holy Office in Rome for suspected heresy (Degert, 1904). The exercise was fraught with difficulties. Fortunately only one of them, Odet de Châtillon, countbishop of Beauvais, was a cardinal. He was the brother of the protestant military leader and admiral of France, Gaspard de Coligny, and his protestantism was largely a matter of clan loyalties. He had never been tonsured and was already openly married in 1563, but, despite the case against him, he continued to enjoy the ample revenues of his diocese until his flight to England in 1568. Among the bishops, some enjoyed powerful political protection for their open toleration of the reform and remained in their sees. Claude Régin, bishop of Oloron, for example, was chancellor to the queen of Navarre in a Béarn diocese and could not be removed.

Jean de Monluc, brother of the formidable royal lieutenant in Gascony, was a favourite with Catherine de Médicis. A great believer in the virtues of eclecticism, he introduced Calvinist prayers and a protestant baptismal service into his diocese and renounced the doctrine of transubstantiation. It is hardly surprising that his diocese of Valence became a favoured watering-hole for Rhône Calvinists. The remainder chose notoriety rather than protection. Jean de Lattes, for example, bishop of Montauban, ran off with his mistress to Geneva, selling his benefices and investing the proceeds in a delightful palace beside Lake Geneva. Jean de St-Chamand, seigneur de St Romain and archbishop of Aix, chose the Christmas Mass of 1566 to denounce the papacy from his pulpit, threw away his cross and mitre and left the town to join the Calvinist army, becoming the most able military commander in lower Languedoc in the 1570s. Perhaps the saddest case though is that of Antonio Caracciolo, bishop of Troyes, who returned from the colloquy of Poissy to his bishopric and presented himself before an astonished consistory, asking to be accepted as a minister (Galpern, 1976, pp. 117–22). After the obligatory period in Geneva, he returned to Troyes, claiming to be 'bishop and minister of the Holy Gospels' thus neatly offending everyone in the city, from which he had shortly to retire in disgrace. The post-Tridentine papacy was not able to exercise much more than a nominal control over appointments to senior clergy before the end of the sixteenth century, but there would be no more embarrassing apostasies. It no longer looked worth it.

Noble support for French protestantism has been called the 'keystone' of the French reformation (Romier, 1925, vol. ii, pp. 255–62). Unfortunately, the judicial records give an inaccurate picture of it, partly because nobles were not often cited before criminal chambers and also because, unlike the first estate, their influence became more important in the period after rather than before 1559. We are, therefore, forced to rely on more impressionistic evidence and individual example, and it is difficult to get an overall view. The role of the nobility in the founding of Calvinist churches was certainly not insignificant even at an early stage. Among the 42 Calvinist ministers sent to France before 1563 whose social status is identifiable, a third (14) were of noble birth (Kingdon,

1956, p. 6). Not all nobles were of equal pedigree, however, in sixteenth-century France. Among these ministers, for example, was Pierre d'Airebaudouze from Anduze who requested to become an inhabitant of Geneva in 1553 and who was classed as a nobleman. Looking more closely, though, one finds that his grandfather was a prosperous draper who had acquired his noble title as co-seigneur of Lésan and baron of Anduze (the gateway to the Cévennes) from a relative who was a rich stocking-maker from the same town (Chassin du Guerny and Gennes, 1978, pp. 211–26). Pierre was an archdeacon of the cathedral in Nîmes before he escaped (without his father's consent) to Geneva. He later returned to be a pastor in Lyon, Montpellier and Nîmes, marrying the daughter of the royal judge there. His sister, Isabel, married another nobleman, a *valet de chambre* of the young king Charles IX, who was also a businessman in the salt pans on the Languedoc coast. His elder brother became a royal judge in Montpellier's financial courts. All the members of the family were protestants and all counted themselves as nobles. They became vital figures in the finances and administration of the Huguenot cause in the region during the civil wars. One cannot explain the influence of the Huguenot cause without the contribution of talents like these; but it is often impossible or artificial to distinguish between what French historians often rather arbitrarily divide into 'old' and 'new' nobility.

Some urban churches enjoyed the protection of the nobility. That of Paris was founded in 1555, thanks to the influence of a nobleman from the Maine, the sieur de Ferrières, who wanted his son christened according to Calvinist rites (Potter and Greengrass, 1983, p. 153). In Tours, the Calvinists were protected by Martin Piballeau, seigneur of a small fief some eight miles from the town (Chevalier, 1985, p. 169). Inevitably, though, it was on the estates of influential landowners and seigneurs who counted for something in regional society that 'squirarchical protestantism' would become more of a reality, at least in the sense of the nomination of ministers and the setting of an example to the tenantry (Garrisson-Estèbe, 1980, pp. 22–8). It was rarely the case, however, that a seigneur paid a minister's salary and even rarer, before 1598, for him to build a protestant church when there was still the possibility that the catholic establishment and tithes could be appropriated to that end.

The motives for noble acceptance of protestantism are often unclear although its reality is undisputed. The French provincial nobility was not as hermetically sealed off from the outside world as is often supposed. Some nobles attended universities where protestant heresy was prevalent; others were influenced by their military service in Italy or in Germany during the Habsburg–Valois wars. Nor should we underestimate the importance of the networks of blood, kinship, feudal and service ties – in short the whole range of noble sociability – which linked the provincial nobility to the court and the high aristocracy. Protestantism grafted itself on to these networks like a new vine on to old stock – newly expressed faith reinforcing old-established fidelities.

We may illustrate this from one example of a noble family of old pedigree from the rolling countryside of the Beauce, north of Orléans (Constant, 1981, pp. 323–4). At the beginning of the century, Jean d'Aussy, *chevalier*, seigneur de Coutures, was a respected captain of a company of *lansquenets* and related by distant cousinage to the famous house of Bourbon-Condé. The Condé family had fallen from favour, following the disgrace and execution of the constable de Bourbon in 1527, but the fidelity of the d'Aussy to the Condé clan remained undiminished. Jean's son was already a captain of a company of *ritters* serving in the French army in 1540 and he followed Louis de Condé into protestantism before the outbreak of the civil wars in 1562. This did not stop the family concluding marriage alliances with catholic families well into the latter half of the sixteenth century for, like many, the d'Aussy wanted to hedge their bets and they considered their loyalty more important than their faith. Jean's grandson, Achille, was later killed at the battle of Ivry in 1589 sounding the bugle for François de Coligny d'Andelot's company, while Achille's younger brother became a captain of the guards protecting the king of Navarre's protestant sister, Catherine de Bourbon. The fourth generation of d'Aussy also served in the French royal armies in the 1620s in the company of the prince of Condé, and one was sent to negotiate with the north German protestant princes in 1629 to try to detach them from the emperor. Here were four generations of loyalty to the Bourbon family, the French army and diplomacy that intravenously and inconspicuously became permeated by pro-testantism.

Behind the family strategies of the French nobility there often lay a formidable *grande dame*, administering the estates and master-minding the marriages of sons and the division of estates. The role of such women in the spread of noble protestantism cannot be ignored, and examples abound from the high aristocracy downwards ('Coligny', 1974, pp. 227–49). We have already touched on the importance of Marguerite d'Angoulême, but there were other protestant *femmes fortes* of her generation such as the constable's sister, Louise de Montmorency, or Henry II's sister, Marguerite de France, whose university in Bourges became a refuge for protestants and who protected Michel de l'Hôpital as the chancellor of the duchy of Berry in the 1550s (Salmon, 1975, pp. 120–1). Among the provincial nobility, Antoine de Pons, who possessed considerable estates in Saintonge, was con-verted by his wife, Anne de Parthenay-Soubise, and his château became yet another protestant stronghold. In Lan-guedoc, Charles de Crussol, viscount of Uzès and possessor of seigneurial rights in over 40 communities of lower Langue-doc, was converted through his marriage to Jeanne de Gen-ouillac from the household of Marguerite d'Angoulême. As seneschal of Nîmes his influence was important in the con-version to protestantism of the royal judges there. Their offspring – Jeanne d'Albret, Louis de Condé, Antoine de Crussol for example – were brought up in a protestant environment, and would be the heroes (and casualties) of the civil wars.

As protestantism got drawn into French noble sensibilities it also had to adapt to clan rivalries, feuds and traditions of violence which were already latent before 1562, but which would emerge during the civil wars. The rivalry between the houses of Montmorency and Guise is perhaps the best documented, and the political origins of the French civil wars have been analysed simply in terms of that rivalry by Lucien Romier (1913, 2 vols). It went on at many levels – in court and council, in the army, in foreign policy, in regional affili-ation and in the pursuit of patronage and honour. The rivalry was at its most bitter in the army, with the constable Anne de Montmorency heading what was known as the *armée militaire*, or the regular army of standing companies of men at arms (*gens d'ordonnance*) and legions of foot in the overall command of the French marshals (*maréchaux*). Although members of the house of Guise had companies of men at arms, not one became a marshal in the regular army before 1589. Instead, as the Grand Master of France, François, duke of Guise, was head of the military household (*maison militaire*), a post of the royal chamber commanding the extensive forces of cavalry and guards of the Valois royal house. With the constable defeated and captured by the Habsburgs at St Quentin in 1557 and the duke of Guise the hero of the capture of Calais in 1558, the stage was set after the peace of Câteau-Cambrésis for the regular army to be stood down, often with arrears of pay unsettled since the royal treasury was exhausted. The festering quarrels between the younger members of the two houses would then break out into the open and take on confessional colours; the Guise from the catholic frontier lands of Champagne and Lorraine supporting militant catholicism, and the Châtillon an aggressive Calvinism.

On the basis of this rivalry it has sometimes been asserted that half the French nobility turned protestant in the 1560s, but this is an exaggeration. In some regions, such as the Beauce, it is possible that up to 40 per cent of the nobility gradually allied with the protestant cause, but many remained uncommitted in the first decade of the civil wars. These were the neutral ones (*casaniers*) who prudently wanted to wait and see what happened. In the diary of a squire from the Cotentin peninsula of Normandy, the sire de Gouberville, we have the record of a wavering catholic (Foisil, 1981, pp. 99–103). In 1562, his attendance at Mass declined and, as news of the popular disturbances which heralded the decline into civil war flooded in, he recorded an anxious conversation as he walked across his acres about the need for 'a new God who would be neither papist nor Huguenot, so that none would say any longer that this God was Lutheran and that one was papist, this one heretic, that one Huguenot'. But Gouberville, echoing Ezekiel, wrote: 'We cannot make Gods because we are only men.' Having attended one protestant sermon in Bayeux at Pentecost 1562, he was shamed into forgetting his feud with the local royal lieutenant and making an appearance at the royalist (and catholic) assembly of the local nobility; he never toyed with the new religion again although he refused to fight it either. If we had more diaries like this, we could make more sense of the varied and contradictory responses of the French nobility to the unfamiliarities of religious pluralism.

Protestantism in the Towns

Sixteenth-century French protestantism has been called an 'urban religion', and it is true that protestants formed a sizeable minority in some towns in the 1560s and the overwhelming majority in a few. All estimates should be treated with suspicion, but the majority were already protestant in the 1560s in such towns as La Rochelle (just over half the population of 25,000 were protestant, according to the baptismal records of 1564), Montpellier and Nîmes (an overwhelming majority). Among those with a substantial minority we should include Lyon (never more than a third of its population), Amiens and Paris (between 10 and 20 per cent) (Lamet, 1978, pp. 35–6). Protestantism thus divided the urban world of sixteenth-century France. Which parts of it were more likely to turn to the new religion?

Imagine yourself in the elaborate urban environment of an early modern town. You would quickly come to recognize the various districts (*quartiers*) of the city which had a formal function in the governing of the city but which also reflected their individual social composition. You would know the cathedral quarter, the market area, the university precincts. Individual streets were the focus for particular artisan activities, often reflected in their names. The architecture of the recently constructed smart town houses in robust stone would tell you that you were in the mercantile heart of the town; you would quickly come to know the area where foreign merchants resided, such as the Florentines in Lyon, the English in Rouen, or the Catalans in Toulouse. Your district would probably be identified by the gate or bridge adjacent to it which you might be required to guard or maintain – an expensive business; all France's cities sought to maintain their defences – and in the process their identity – in the sixteenth century. Outside the gates, you would recognize the suburbs (*faubourgs*) and look down on their inhabitants – many of them recent migrants from the countryside around, working in the town but unable to call themselves 'bourgeois'; magistrates regarded the *faubourgs* as the source for most social evils. A permanent migration from the surrounding countryside was vital to sustain this expanding urban population in its fundamentally unhealthy environment. There was little privacy in an early modern French city; streets turned into back alleys and domestic quarrels and conversations spilled out from houses into streets. All but the merchants and royal officials, who were in the process of building themselves houses around an inner courtyard, enjoyed a neighbourly sociability which we would regard now as intrusive. In this extensive public space, traditional religion had an accepted place. The geography (street, hill, waterfront, fountain, bridge, river, parish church, cemetery, hospital) had corresponding religious rituals in the routes of processions, the meeting points for fraternities, the beatings of bounds, the holding of elections. Religious buildings shared and were invaded by secular functions and concerns; feasts took place in cemeteries, churches were used for local meetings, pedlars sold their candles and votive offerings alongside the purveyors of second-hand furniture or pornographic books in cathedral precincts, even in their porches. The calendar of each district was dominated by the irregular celebration of feasts for patron saints as well as the great moments of Carnival and Lent which were the fixed points of catholic sociability (Davis, 1981).

The new religion was bound to be deeply divisive of this urban environment. Protestantism was identified with particular *quartiers* of individual cities. In Paris, the Latin quarter of the left bank and the prosperous merchant parts of the *quartier* St-Germain were known points of secret protestant worship; 130 were arrested on 4 September 1557 when a night-time meeting of the protestants in Paris was surprised by students in the rue St-Jacques of the Latin quarter (Richet, 1977, p. 765). In Caen, the equivalent was the *quartier* St-Jean where the noble and bourgeois families from the rue St-Jean gathered to hear Beza's sermons in 1563; but there were also many protestants in the populous inner city parishes

(Lamet, 1978, pp. 40–1; c.f. Benedict, 1981, ch. iii). In Tours, the new religion was identified with the quarter to the west of the city near the *Halles* and around the *tour* Feu-Hugon; several independent contemporary sources tell us that the word Huguenot originated there in the 1550s to describe those suspected protestants who inhabited this particular part of the city (Gray, 1983, pp. 354–7). The war on the streets of Toulouse in May 1562 took place between the protestant areas (around the university colleges, the town hall, and the artisan neighbourhood near the river Garonne) on the one side, and the royal officials' quarter (around the *parlement* and cathedral) on the other (Greengrass, 1983).

Urban protestantism could call on support both among the city notables (*gens de bien*) and the artisans and lower orders (*menu peuple*). The proscription lists for Toulouse, Grenoble and Montpellier (see appendix) indicate that between 55 and 65 per cent of those suspected of protestantism in the 1560s were 'notables'. Within these broad categories, however, certain groups responded more positively to the new religion than others. The reasons in each case take us to the frontiers of current research and hypothesis.

Merchants, for example, were present more often than bankers or financiers. The protestants of Paris had a disproportionately high number of sympathizers and active adherents among the 200 families engaged in the international commerce of the capital (Richet, 1977, p. 767). In Lyon, the financial capital of France before 1560, Italian bankers remained loyal to catholicism and the monarchy, while the merchants veered towards protestantism. Was it the case that the skein of debts owed to the former by the French monarchy kept them orthodox whereas the trading contacts of the latter with protestant powers abroad gave them more of a taste for the protestant religion? Did they respond more warmly to protestant sanctification of work and the need for an inner discipline, its elimination of saints' day feasts and the disorder of carnival? Antoine de Marcourt, in his *Book of the Merchants*, had compared the catholic clergy with their money-changing tables in the temple to financiers; by implication, the protestants were the true merchants, their work sanctioned by diligence and purity. The red-letter days of the protestants were evenly spread throughout the year at Christmas, Easter,

Pentecost and September, 'like the fairs of Lyon' as a catholic from the city remarked maliciously (Davis, 1981, p. 62). Did the greater privacy of the new faith accord more neatly with the domesticity which they sought in their urban hôtels, in the secrecy of whose courtyards many early protestant services were first held?

Merchants sought respectability in positions of urban government, which were still relatively open to them since royal officers were often excluded from municipal posts. It is not therefore surprising to find protestants using town halls for the services in 1562 and exploiting the positions of authority which these positions gave them. Catholics became convinced that the ability of the protestants to seize control in several large cities like Rouen, Lyon or Toulouse in 1562 had relied on the active connivance of the city magistrates. The evidence suggests that a minority of town magistrates in the big cities *did* become active protestants, but that it was more among the consuls of the smaller towns (*bourgades*) of the Midi where 'civic protestantism' became a reality (Garrisson-Estèbe, 1980, pp. 31–3). Protestantism undoubtedly gave a greater place to municipal authority. In towns where protestant regimes were established, church wealth was confiscated and inventoried by the town magistrates, and parochial boundaries were scrapped in favour of civic quarters. Municipal consuls also served as the elders on the consistory courts, anxious to enforce godly discipline on their communities. Nowhere were there more *bourgades* than in the Midi; an intendant in Languedoc in the 1640s reckoned that there were about 2,500 communities in that province alone (with perhaps as many as 10,000 elected consuls) (Lublinskaya, 1966, p. 168). With hindsight, we can see that it was in these communities that the self-sustaining power of French protestantism would most powerfully reside. Well before the formal treatises of the right to resist unjust kings were published in the 1570s, catholics claimed that Midi protestantism was but the prelude to the establishment of civil republics. 'They want to set themselves up as a canton like those of Geneva' was how they put it, and perhaps their fear was the deep-seated one that somehow the natural economy of authority among Huguenots, more heavily based on organic self-regulating families, was fundamentally opposed to the

57

natural economy of the catholics with its imposed and ritu-
alized authority of church and state.

It is important, however, to underline the inherent prudence and timidity of those in power in the major cities. Most
notables in city affairs were anxious not to compromise their
brief periods in office and were open to pressure from royal
authority. Only in the third civil war in 1568 did La Rochelle's magistrates decide to support the protestantism of the
majority of its inhabitants (Meyer, 1984, pp. 172–81;
cf. Guggenheim, 1972). Prudence was to an even greater
extent the hallmark of the senior royal judges and officials.
No judge of any *parlement* followed the recklessness of Anne
Du Bourg, who declared his heretical convictions in a speech
before the king in 1559 and, in so doing, signed his own
death warrant. In some tribunals, such as that of Toulouse,
as much as a third of the judges was suspected of protestant
sympathies after the attempted protestant coup of May 1562,
but much of the evidence was circumstantial and probably
fabricated by the factions within the royal officialdom of
the city. Mutual suspicions and antagonisms, as well as the
important investments they had made in their offices, kept
them catholic.

The same constraints did not apply to the legal world which
inhabited the lobbies (*parquets*) of the law courts. Advocates,
attorneys and notaries were, along with physicians and sur-
geons, professors and teachers, musicians and book-sellers,
the constituent elements of what have been classed as the
'liberal professions'. The appendix indicates how important
the thinking and communicating groups of people in French
towns were to the spread of French protestantism. The notaries (often serving as town clerks as well) acted as lightning
conductors bringing the new faith to earth in their communities. We must not underestimate the extent to which it was
intellectually 'smart' to profess protestantism among these
groups on the eve of the civil wars; as Donald Kelley has
argued, its dialectic and vocabulary suited their education,
interests and social functions – what he calls their 'con-
sciousness' (1981, chs iv–v). When the king set up new
benches of lesser judges (*présidiaux*) in 1552, some of this
group purchased offices in them which may in part explain
why this generation of officeholders in places like Dax,

Saintes, Béziers and Nîmes disregarded their investment in office and followed their consciences.

The influence of protestantism among certain groups of artisans was evident from an early stage. At Meaux, it was the enthusiasms of the the textile workers which most alarmed the *parlement* of Paris in the 1520s; in Paris, the dyers and combers; in Lyon, the silk-workers and printers. Henri Hauser wrote of the reformation by 1560 as the 'working man's cause', but different craft groups reacted differently (Hauser, 1899, p. 31). Generally speaking, protestantism made a good showing among the artisans of leather, metal, paper and cloth. It did conspicuously poorly in those of food, wood, brick, stone and mortar. Three hypotheses – those of literacy, industrial adversity and craft novelty – have been used to explain this divergence, but none of them seems a wholly satisfying answer in itself. It was obviously the case that literacy rates varied dramatically from craft to craft, and between artisans and peasant labourers. 'Huguenot carders and Papist peasants' was how the historian of Languedoc's peasantry summarized it, pointing out the correlation between artisans with some literary dexterity (crudely measured by the ability to sign one's name) and their protestant affiliation (Le Roy Ladurie, 1974, pp. 152–64). But the correlation is not an exact one. The protestant shoemakers of Nîmes had a low rate of literacy, and the protestant weavers of Amiens were no better endowed with writing skills than were other groups of workers there among whom protestantism made less headway (Rosenberg, 1978, pp. 40–62). There were, in any case, so many ways by which protestantism could be caught other than from the pages of a book that this explanation looks too simplistic.

It used to be said, when it was fashionable to find purely materialist explanations for social movements, that industrial adversity in particular trades explains why their practitioners turned to protestantism. The explanation has an enduring and basic plausibility to it, for we know that wage rates were declining quite rapidly in the middle decades of the century and that artisans often found themselves in a very vulnerable position within their crafts, under pressure from an oligarchy of merchants from above and competition from journeymen below. There were a number of strikes in various trades to prove the point, of which the most advertised was that of the printing workers of Lyon in the 1540s. Investigating this strike in the context of the growth of protestantism, Natalie Davis concluded that protestant journeymen, artisans and merchants tended to be grouped together in the same printing outfits, despite the industrial disputes, and that there was no evidence that the guilds and fraternities of the printing workers were nascent protestant communities (Davis, 1975, ch. i). Protestantism was not the religion of industrial resentment. This led her to propose a third form of explanation, that of the novelty of the craft skills and the willingness of its workers therefore to contemplate change. She found that, in Lyon, there was a significant correlation between the newer trades – such as silk manufacture, gun- and metal-working, and printing – and protestantism. Further, that protestantism was more prevalent among recent migrants to the city than long-established residents (Davis, 1981). Protestantism found its recruits among those artisans least committed to established patterns of work, leisure (and, thus, of religion) in their environment. The hypothesis certainly makes sense of the adherence of the textile workers in the production of new draperies (*sayetterie*) in northern France. It is not applicable on the other hand to the leather trades, the silver- and goldsmiths and other well-established crafts which lent their support to protestantism in large numbers.

There is a danger, in any case, of becoming too surgical in our analysis and forgetting that, when artisans embraced the new faith, they did so with a violent and proud enthusiasm, rather than a cool and dispassionate conviction. From the records of municipal jurisdictions, where the cases of slander, theft and petty crime among artisans were most frequently dealt with, we have the richest images of the world of the sixteenth-century craftsman. The artisan is neighbourly yet quarrelsome, protective of the honour of his trade, his family and his kin, violent and vocal, proud of his independence and skills, exploiting to the full the dense public space of early modern cities. His moral values are clear and unshaded – 'he' is a 'thief' and a 'liar' (*larron, menteur*), 'I' am a 'worthy man' (*homme de bien*). In court rooms, before patient city notables (and later before Calvinist consistories too), we glimpse a world in which literacy, industrial protest and new craft skills are part of a mentality of artisan protestantism – iconoclastic, egalitarian, in which the black and white of protestant and catholic would find a place. 'The prayers of a layman are as good as those of a priest', said a protestant weaver at a guild banquet in Amiens in 1564; 'In church ... there is no head save Jesus Christ ... the least person is equal to the greatest; all are equal.' Beware the weavers of Amiens, 'prompt to mutiny when one touches, be it ever so slightly, on their interests', said a contemporary, and the printers of Lyon had a similarly violent reputation. It is easy to imagine how sectarian riots became a tragic feature of French cities in the civil wars.

Protestantism and the Rural World

The majority of Frenchmen still lived on the land. If the peasantry had looked as though it would be untouched by the reformation, then the protestants should have been resigned to the frustration of a fringe existence in French society from the start. But things did not look like that, at least not in the 'wonder-years' of 1561–2. There were, after all, a large number of peasants who worked in towns or who lived in the *faubourgs*; up to half of the 10,000 or so people in Nîmes, according to one calculation, were, in reality, day-labourers from the nearby countryside. They would not be impervious to protestant evangelization, even if it was slower to take root than among artisan inhabitants. In addition, in some localities, seigneurial protestantism succeeded in creating, perforce, a Huguenot peasantry. There were also those regions where the networks of rural industry created a dispersed protestantism, such as the Cévennes (Le Roy Ladurie, 1974, pp. 164–71). The traditional church was undoubtedly weak in resources and adaptability in the rural world, and it is not surprising that protestants should have expected a response from what is often called 'la France profonde'.

The response, however, was always a limited one. Even in the Cévennes or the Béarn Pyrenees, valley rivalries interspersed catholic and Huguenot settlements on alternate hillsides (Joutard, 1979, pp. 110–11). In some localities, protestantism seems to have fuelled anti-seigneurial movements, and the murder of the baron Fumel in cold blood in Guyenne on the eve of the civil wars, as well as anti-noble movements in

Normandy, were cited by catholics as signs that protestantism would bring with it class war (*Histoire ecclésiastique*, vol. i, pp. 789; 856; 885–6; Nicholls, 1980, p. 295). Refusal to pay tithes (which was widespread during the first civil wars) also came into this category, the problem for the catholic church being aggravated by the fact that many of its tithe farmers were also Huguenots. But the Calvinist church was clear that tithes were a legitimate exaction and merely wished to appropriate them to pay for their own ministers (Le Roy Ladurie, 1974, pp. 181–90).

At the heart of the failure of the protestant church to convert the rural world to the new faith lay a failure of mission and evangelization. It could not overcome the problem of illiteracy; there were never enough ministers and established churches; there was never any effort to preach and catechize in anything but French in a rural world which was dominated by *patois*. The wars of religion diverted resources and drained the enthusiasm among French protestants for peaceful mission and conversion. In any case, the experience of protestant implantation elsewhere in Europe in the sixteenth century suggests that it would be heavily dependent on the full cooperation of the state; whether the Huguenots would achieve that was a question answered in the French civil wars.

4 The Huguenots and the Civil Wars

Writing to the Swiss legation then in Paris, the clandestine protestant church in the capital reported its gathering momentum in the wake of the affair in the rue St-Jacques in 1557. Despite its shaky beginning, God had given it his blessing ('Deo gratia et placentia'); by his providence, the harvest for Christ was nowhere more prolific. In good conscience and desiring to do his works, they rejoiced in the protection of the Almighty while they were, like Daniel, in the 'lion's mouth' (Aubert, 1947, pp. 101–2). Orthodox French Calvinists interpreted what happened to them in biblical and providential terms. This is important for an understanding of the oscillation between confidence and fatalism which is at the heart of Huguenot reaction to the tragic events of the French civil wars.

Prelude to Civil War

The Huguenots could have been forgiven for imagining in the months of 1561 and early 1562 that the complete reformation of France was about to take place, albeit in a chaotic and disordered fashion. With official repression on the wane, congregations were growing rapidly. 'We have, thanks to God, churches in nearly all the cities of the realm, and soon there will be scarcely a place where one has not been established' wrote Jean Morély, sire de Villiers in 1562 (Morély, 1968, pp. 54–5). He was an active protestant whose controversial treatise on the organization of the church (*Traicté de la discipline & police Chrestienne*) proposed that authority should reside with protestant congregations rather than with the consistories; it reflected the confidence of French protestantism at its period of greatest growth, just as its condemnation later in the decade by national synods reinforced the more austere, consistorial and Genevan form of protestantism which suited a minority church feeling itself under threat (Kingdon, 1967). He described the printing press as 'Truth's triumphal chariot' and perhaps the most famous publication of these years was the book of psalms by Clément Marot, completed by Theodore Beza and produced by Antoine Vincent, a rich merchant-publisher from Lyon (Berthoud, 1957, pp. 276–93). In exile in Geneva, Vincent master-minded one of sixteenth-century Europe's most ambitious publishing ventures. He commissioned 27,400 copies from the Genevan presses alone in 1562; others were printed in Lyon, Orléans, Metz, Poitiers and St Lô. The sound of these psalms being sung in the streets of Rouen, in the sun-drenched squares of Toulouse, and countless other urban settings during the summer of 1561, was (for catholics) the menacing public face of the blossoming new faith.

It was almost impossible not to prevent the new religion turning into an assault on catholic property and values. As the *cahier* from the town of Nîmes to the estates-general planned for May 1561 said: 'those who cannot in good conscience accept the ceremonies of the Roman church should be given means to be instructed and taught the word of God' – the means being churches and revenues. Wherever catholic churches were taken over in 1561–2, popular image-breaking was likely to take place. It proved impossible for the protestant ministers to enforce Calvin's demand that, where relics and images were removed, they should be carefully inventoried and stored by the town magistrates. French iconoclasm was less organized and systematic than that of the Low Countries in 1566, but it doubtless contributed to a similar sense of imminent triumph among its participants. The poetry and prints of the period capture something of the protestant mood. In a Calvinist poem, published in Lyon in 1561 as the *Muster of the Archers at the Popinjay* (*La Monstre des Archers au Papegay*), the artisans of the watch and ward, led by Calvin and Viret, take pot-shots at the catholic target (popinjay) and enjoy watching it topple (Pineaux, 1971, pp. 80–1). In a widely circulated and well-known woodcut, entitled *The Great Marmite Overturned* (*La Grande Marmite Renversée*), the pope and his minions are shown trying to prop up the wealth and possessions of the church (in the form of a great stew-pot) whilst the light of the Holy Gospel inspires the common people to cast it down. These were the years of the protestant church militant.

The Huguenots were also engaged in organizing national petitions and exerting political pressure on both the enfeebled government of the young king Francis II (1559–60), and then on the minority of his brother Charles IX (1560–3). By the edict of Amboise of March 1560, the government more or less admitted that persecution of protestants had become unenforcible (Sutherland, 1980, pp. 347–8). In the same month, according to the moderate, official account of the confusing events known as the 'Conspiracy of Amboise' put before the *parlement* of Paris, a national rally to present the Huguenot faith at court was overshadowed by a noble conspiracy which implicated the prince of Condé (Poujol, 1973, p. 171). Further national petitions (*remonstrances*) were prepared by the Huguenots in April and May 1560, and we may presume that they also exploited the calling of the estates-general to Orléans in December 1560 to advance their cause. In May 1561, the deputies to the second national synod in Poitiers drew up a further petition to put before the king's advisers. Protestant demands at this time were straightforward: they wanted the dismantling of machinery of repression against heresy, the right to worship in their churches openly, and the summoning of a 'holy and free' council to reform the church to which they would send deputies on an equal footing with the catholics (Sutherland, 1984, ch. vii).

How close did they come to achieving their aims before the fracture of the French polity in the first civil war in April 1562? Their first request was substantially accepted by the regency government of Catherine de Médicis. By letters issued under her private seal (*lettres de cachet*) of 28 January 1561, all those imprisoned on religious grounds were released and all heresy cases suspended (Sutherland, 1980, pp. 351–2). Royal courts were still expected to enforce the laws against sedition, and the edict of 20 October 1561 decreed the death penalty for all those guilty of iconoclasm or the seizure of churches. The second demand was squeezed from the regency government in a highly modified form in the first of what have become known as the edicts of toleration. The edict of St-Germain-en-Laye (17 January 1562), issued on the eve of the civil wars, granted protestants provisional and conditional permission to meet for public worship outside towns, unarmed, by day, and under the supervision of royal officials (Sutherland, 1980, pp. 354–6). Money-raising, printing, preaching and the holding of synods, however, were still either banned or carefully circumscribed. Their third demand for the holding of a council (the protestants called it a colloquy (*colloque*)) was met by the notorious conference of Poissy in September 1561. There, Theodore Beza from Geneva led the protestant delegation to present the Calvinist confession to the assembled catholic delegates who were led by the cardinal of Lorraine. The meeting was, as N.M. Sutherland has shown, the apotheosis of the cardinal's political skills and suppleness (1984, ch. vii). He had wanted a council to reform the church, similar to that which Henry II had summoned in 1551 in the face of the decision to reconvene the council of Trent. He had not wanted a colloquy with the protestants on an equal footing; when that became inevitable in the turmoil of the summer of 1561, he fought to ensure that the protestant delegation was there only to present its views, rather than shape the future destiny of the church in France.

At the colloquy itself, the chief point of contention became the 'Real Presence'. The cardinal of Lorraine proposed that, if the protestant delegation formally committed itself to a Lutheran formulation on the sacraments, this *might* (and he carefully refused to sign anything himself) form the basis for an acceptable compromise on which the Gallican church could unite. The offer was a personal one and, amidst the tensions and fears of the moment, it was unlikely that he would have carried a majority of the senior French clergy or the Sorbonne with him. As Calvin wrote to Beza, reflecting the natural suspicions of the Calvinist theologians: 'Believe me, the bishops will never proceed to a serious discussion' (Potter and Greengrass, 1983, p. 167). The colloquy broke up without agreement; although protestants continued to press for the holding of another, this was, in reality, the last time that a 'Gallican' solution to France's sectarian problem would be seriously considered. The civil wars broke out in April 1562 with the prince of Condé setting up the protestant headquarters in Orléans on 2 April and issuing a formal declaration of war, or *Protestation* a week later (Kelley, 1981, pp. 255–7). They were fighting, he declared, for the 'matter of religion', given the failure of the edict of toleration, and for the political rights of princes of the blood. He stressed their loyalty towards the king, the queen mother and his elder brother, the first prince of the blood. But the aim of the civil war, however it was dressed up, was to seize power.

Edicts of Toleration

What chance had the Huguenots of capturing the state by military force? Given that we know the outcome of the story, it is easy for us to read history backwards and to conclude that the Huguenots were bound to fail. To avoid this, let us speculate briefly on what might have happened had the Huguenots gained the upper-hand, militarily speaking, in the first war of religion from 1562–3. Suppose, for example, that the city of Rouen had withstood the siege by royal forces in October 1562 and that the battle of Dreux, just outside a small town in Normandy beside the shallow river Eure, had been won by the protestant forces on 19 December 1562 and that Orléans had not therefore been besieged in February 1563. These would have been the constituent elements of a protestant military victory in the first civil war.

The assumptions are not inherently or completely implausible. Rouen was a notoriously difficult city to besiege, protected on one side by the river Seine and on the other by a hill with an almost inaccessible fortress on the summit. The city could be counted on to provide stubborn resistance, for it had a large protestant minority, and there was an English expeditionary force landing in nearby Le Havre as well as a large reserve of English money for troops stored in Dieppe, ready to assist the protestants (Benedict, 1981, pp. 98–101). In addition, the autumn had been appallingly wet and the royal camp was rife with fever. The commander of the royal troops, Antoine de Bourbon, was wounded in the shoulder by a stray bullet in the course of the siege, and it was only a singularly determined Catherine de Médicis who rallied the army. She delivered a speech to them about how her young son, their king, was not to be left to the mercy of English traitors and ordered the bombardment of 10,000 cannon-shot under which the fortress at Rouen collapsed on 28 October 1562. The battle of Dreux was even less a foregone conclusion. The main body of royal troops was routed by a well-led and organized protestant army, raised partly through protestant churches and partly through the established fidelities to the protestant princes, led by Condé and the admiral de Coligny. The leaders of the royal army – the constable de Mont-morency and the marshal de St-André – were both wounded. As the enemy fled in disorder, the protestants rested for a few moments in the village of Blainville and it was during this brief respite that the household troops of the duke of Guise were able to bear down on them and win the day. Had the battle of Dreux not been lost, 2,000 protestant German mercenaries would not have surrendered and the protestant army would have looked invincible; the siege of Orléans would never have taken place. As it was, Orléans, where the protestants under the prince of Condé had raised their stan-dard in April 1562, became the town whose imminent fall a year later signalled the end of formal hostilities and the negotiation of the first edict of pacification in March 1563 at Amboise.

What would a peace settlement have looked like, if the Huguenots had 'won' the first civil war? From the demands in 1561–2 and the edicts of pacification which they accepted subsequently, particularly in August 1570 (the peace of St-German-en-Laye), May 1576 (the peace of Monsieur), Sep-tember 1577 (the peace of Bergerac) and April 1598 (the pacification of Nantes), it is easy to predict that they would have required a public recognition, guaranteed by royal laws, of protestant rights to worship, bury their dead, baptize their children, appoint, pay and hear their preachers, hold their colloquies and conferences and discipline their adherents – in short, a favourable edict of toleration and recognition (Sutherland, 1980, chs v, vii, viii). They might even have persuaded the catholics to allow some guarantees of protestant security in the form of garrisoned strongholds and pensions from the royal treasury for the upkeep of their ministers, such as were part of the pacification of Nantes in 1598. It is unlikely, however, that the catholics would have conceded more, even if the protestants had gained a temporary military superiority. After all, despite the prince of Condé's shrewdness in urging the protestants to seize the major cities of France, only a minority had fallen to the protestants, and Paris, strategically and politically the most important, had eluded them. Catholic consent to the terms of any pacification inevitably meant substantial concessions by the protestants. Calvin intemperately dismissed Condé as 'basely betraying' the movement by the terms of the pacification of Amboise in 1563, but he failed to take account of these realities (Potter and Greengrass, 1983, p. 168).

Edicts of toleration presented a principle which it was difficult for French monarchs to be seen to concede openly. They were Most Christian Kings, and the traditions, rituals and ceremonies of their office were closely linked to the beliefs and practices of the catholic church. There was widespread belief, too, that no realm could be at peace within itself with two religions worshipped simultaneously (a so-called *simultaneum*). On this matter, the views of mainstream catholic opinion were not dissimilar to those of Pierre Viret, protestant minister in Lyon, Nîmes and elsewhere, whose critique of an 'interim' religious settlement which involved the toleration of the two religions until such time in the future as a free and holy general council of the church might reunite them, was published in 1565 and dedicated to the admiral de Coligny (*l'Intérim fait par dialogues ...*). Deputations to court from the provincial estates expressed a similar point of view and so, too, did catholic prelates; the king ignored their opinions at his peril for his government depended on them for large amounts of revenue.

Edicts of toleration were difficult, but not impossible, to justify. There was already the example of the famous *Interim* settlement in the Holy Roman Empire in 1548, modified and eventually accepted as the pacification of Augsburg of 1555. The 'permitting' of another religion could be presented as necessary to the state's survival. The verb 'permettre' (as in the 'permitting' of a privilege) was much more acceptable than the verb 'tolérer' which still carried overtones of the kind of dangerous licence which would lead inevitably to atheism and libertinism, fears of which were often voiced by contemporaries during the civil wars (Huseman, 1984). Classical and early Christian precedents for tolerating minority faiths were put together and wielded with as much conviction as he could muster by Catherine de Médicis' chancellor, Michel de l'Hôpital (1507–73), an elderly, somewhat austere, senior judge (Salmon, 1975, pp. 152–61). He also proposed sweeping changes to the administration of the French state, believing that the civil wars had been caused as much by corruption as by religious discontent. However, he was forced to retire in disgrace from his chancellorship in 1568, hounded out by the opponents of religious toleration and the enemies he had made by his other reforms. His ideas would live on, but his fate was an obvious lesson in the difficulties for those in royal service of accepting Huguenot demands for toleration, even demands as limited as those which were, in reality, granted in the peace of 1563.

Legal Enforcement

Who could the protestants trust to carry out effectively and impartially the requirements of an edict of pacification? Their early experiences were scarcely encouraging. The first edict of St-Germain put the powers of enforcement in the hands of the lesser law courts (*présidiaux*) and town councils in those larger towns where city officials had rights of justice under their charters. But these local agents quickly proved partisan. In some places, the tribunals were completely divided and powerless; in others they were the preserve of catholic or protestant groups. Town councils were also the prey to local factions and, like the *présidiaux*, their authority was questioned and ignored. The 1562 edict, far from being a prelude to the peaceful conversion of many, perhaps the majority, of Frenchmen, instead contributed to the tensions and confusions which led to civil war.

There remained other permanent organs of authority in the provinces to enforce royal will, the *parlements* and the military governors. These were called on to enforce the edict of pacification in 1563 and all subsequent edicts too. The protestants did not welcome the participation of the senior judges, which was hardly surprising given their past history in the suppression of heresy and their known, overwhelmingly catholic, leanings. The judges were largely convinced that protestantism led to sedition and the court in Paris had refused to register the first edict of toleration of January 1562; Catherine de Médicis had to come post haste to the judges to demand their cooperation. In the end, they sanctioned the edict after modifications, but only temporarily until the king came of age. As for the edict of pacification in 1563, their recalcitrance was even more evident: they used every tactic of delay and prevarication to stop it. One reason for the royal progress of 1564–5 was to ensure, by a visit to each *parlement* in turn, that the king showed the judges his determination to be obeyed. Persuading the *parlements* to register edicts of toleration and pacification remained a problem throughout the civil wars. Even with the pacification of Nantes (1598), certain detailed clauses, which might have been open to criticism, were placed in a separate schedule of so-called 'secret' articles which did not require the judges' consent. The concessions on the military strongholds and pensions to Huguenot ministers in 1598 were given under the king's private seal (which meant that their validity only lasted during his lifetime) partly to avoid judicial opposition. Even so, the judges proved obstructive; the *parlement* of Rouen succeeded in resisting the complete acceptance of its terms until 1609. It is not surprising, therefore, that protestants doubted whether the judges would enforce it fairly and demanded the creation of separate chambers in the *parlements* (*chambres mi-parties*), where protestants (not always half the bench of judges as the name suggests) would sit alongside catholics to hear cases of those who adhered to the reformed faith. A minority of hard-line catholic magistrates became politically engaged and actively promoted local catholic leagues to eradicate protestantism, by force if necessary. Their presence in these leagues legitimized, and thus increased the risk of, an organized catholic backlash during the civil wars, such as would occur under the catholic League.

Could the protestants rely on the military wing of the provincial administration – the governors, lieutenants, troops of cavalry and garrisons – to protect them? The answer depended on the province in question. A number of royal garrison commanders turned to the new religion and were in a position to shelter it. But among the provincial governors, only the Bourbon princes – Louis, prince of Condé, in Picardy and his brother, Antoine de Bourbon, king of Navarre, governor of Guyenne – did so for any length of time before 1589. For a variety of reasons, neither they nor their offspring were able to turn these provinces into safe havens for protestants. For the rest of the provincial governors, the degree to which they were prepared to protect protestants depended on the politics of the moment. It is not surprising that the Huguenots demanded various garrisoned strongholds (*places de sûreté*) as part of the edicts of pacification from 1570 onwards. If the Huguenots had won a substantial military victory at an early stage, it is possible to imagine that there might have been more aristocratic conversions to the new faith and a greater feeling of confidence in the degree of security which governors could provide. On the other hand, these posts, while theoretically held in commission, were generally the fiefs of noble families, and whoever had won the civil war would have had to work for the foreseeable future with catholic nobles, many of whom were suspicious of the intentions of protestants in impregnable positions of military importance in the provinces.

Protestants and Political Influence

Difficulties enforcing the royal edicts of pacification led the protestants to rely to a greater extent on royal protection. In 1564 and 1565, those provinces in which the protestants were strong sent back detailed and substantial complaints to the royal council of the inadequacies of the edict of pacification in their localities. The council responded by sending commissioners, known as masters of requests (*maîtres des requêtes*), to investigate the complaints and report back to them (Garrisson, 1950). These were senior lawyers, experienced administrators, patient investigators and often close friends of the four secretaries of the royal chancery (*chancellerie du roi*), better known as the secretaries of state. Each secretary was responsible for handling the business of a group of provinces before the royal councils; they were, like the masters of requests, immensely experienced and resourceful administrators, capable, if any were, of making the French state work, even in the most difficult circumstances (Sutherland, 1962). After each edict, the royal council continued to dispatch commissioners to enforce its will and to engage in the often laborious and detailed business of peace-making. Their experience of where the difficult problems lay and how they might be resolved contributed to the formulation of better legislation. This group of moderate catholics was important in bringing the wars of religion to a close and ensuring that protestant rights were respected. They included such figures as the famous historian of the civil wars, Jacques-Auguste de Thou, and Michel Hurault de l'Hôpital, grandson of Catherine's chancellor whose reputation both did much to reinstate. They are sometimes called 'politiques', although they belonged to no formal party beyond the king's. Here, however, was a paradox for the protestants. The more the protestants relied on civil war to protect their cause, the greater they weakened royal authority and the less effective it was in delivering what they wanted. If the protestants had won the civil wars, would the king not have lost? Would his commissioners then have been obeyed?

The king's council had a special and intricate relationship with the royal court. The princes of the blood and pre-eminent aristocrats sometimes attended the various councils, and even when not attending they made sure their views were clearly expressed in the corridors of power. What chance was there that the protestants could 'dominate' at court in this period? The factional politics of the French court were sophisticated, mercurial and baffling even to experienced contemporary observers. Anything could happen and the few formal conventions did not count for much. In theory, for example, there were customs to be observed in the case of a royal minority or young king who had yet to assume the fullness of authority; but the protestants would have been the first to recall with bitterness how these conventions could be set aside. Following the death of Henry II in 1559, the kingdom had passed into the hands of his eldest son, Francis II, who was 15 years old. This meant that he was a major since, by French law and custom, majority occurred at the age of 14 or during the fourteenth year. But he had not yet attained plenitude of power – this would occur when he was 21. He was still required to take the advice of a council of protection on matters of state and those affecting the royal inheritance. Following many precedents, the queen mother played a major role during his tutelage and the council should have been led by the senior prince of the blood – in 1559, this was Antoine de Bourbon, king of Navarre. In reality, Francis II was easily dominated by François de Lorraine, duke of Guise, the hero of the hour after his victory at Calais in 1558. Protestants were excluded from favour and influence. Louis, prince of Condé, was arraigned for high treason for alleged participation in the noble conspiracy of Amboise in March 1560, whilst his elder brother Antoine undoubtedly lay behind another major attempted conspiracy in the summer of 1560, which never reached fruition (Dufour, 1963, 269–80). Calvin refused to support the former, but gave his backing (even acting as financial agent) to the latter. In his eyes, there was a world of difference between the illegitimacy of a rebellion, even if in a good cause, and the legitimacy of a loyal revolt led by the senior prince of the blood, like the king of Navarre, who was being denied his lawful rights by tyranny. Protestants claimed to have a just cause against tyranny and this was the theme of François Hotman's vigorous and seditious pamphlet against the cardinal of Lorraine and the Guise clan, the *Tiger of France*, published in Strasburg in the summer of 1560 (Kelley, 1973, pp. 99–129).

Francis II died suddenly in December 1560 and was succeeded by his younger brother, Charles IX. This time, it was a genuine minority. Generally speaking, the disposition of power in a minority was governed by the predecessor's will but Francis II had left nothing in his will and so Catherine de Médicis seized power on behalf of her son and proclaimed herself regent. There were precedents for her actions in French history; but a powerful case could be made for the need to summon an estates-general of the kingdom and to call on the princes of the blood to constitute a regency government. Calvin immediately saw the importance of the position and wrote to Antoine de Bourbon from Geneva, urging him to establish a regency council and impose his will at court against that of Catherine (Potter and Greengrass, 1983, p. 167). It was the greatest opportunity the protestants would have before 1589 to 'dominate' the French court. However, Antoine de Bourbon let them down totally (Sutherland, 1984, ch. iv). Charmed by Catherine, he was appointed lieutenant-general of the kingdom, but denied the post of regent. He deserted the protestants and headed the military forces against them in the first civil war. Wounded at the siege of Rouen, he died after accompanying Catherine into the city for a triumphal parade. His wife, Jeanne d'Albret, regent for his patrimony in the south-west of France, refused to go north to tend to him, and he died in the arms of one of Catherine de Médicis' female attendants and his mistress, whom the queen had used as her spy and informant (Roelker, 1968, pp. 199–207). Attended alternately by a Dominican friar and a Huguenot preacher, assuring each in turn that he died in their particular faith, he was not contemptuously called 'the Changeling' (*l'Echangeur*) by the protestants for nothing. The opportunity of 1560–1 was unlikely to recur quickly. In August 1563, Charles IX was (a few months prematurely) granted his majority and for the remainder of his tutelage (that is, until the traditional wedding celebrations and elaborate royal entry to Paris which took place in early 1571), the princes of the blood royal were hostile to the protestants. Huguenot hopes of power lay in the desperate and hopeless expedient of a *coup d'état*.

There was still the possibility that the protestants might be able to win the friendship and favour of Charles IX, once he had achieved mature and absolute authority in the kingdom. This is what the admiral, Gaspard de Coligny, leader of the French protestants after 1569 and, by common consent, one of the most able strategists of his generation, set out to achieve in the years 1571–2. He managed, with the support of his kinsmen, to charm the young king into backing a proposed invasion of the Low Countries. The details of Coligny's strategy need not detain us here, for they have been extensively analysed by N.M. Sutherland (1973). It was a bold plan, diplomatically and militarily coherent. It also made sense as part of the pacification of France, for most contemporaries believed that foreign wars would drain the 'evil humours' from the kingdom 'like waters from a gutter'. It was superficially attractive to the young king, eager to follow in his father's military footsteps and avenge the disaster at St-Quentin. The *rapprochement* between the king and the protestants was cemented by the marriage of Charles IX's sister to the son of Antoine de Bourbon and Jeanne d'Albret, Henri, in August 1572. But Coligny's plans and this marriage alliance placed Charles in a critical and dangerous position at court which, through inexperience, he was incapable of handling. Coligny was assassinated in Paris on 17 August 1572 by members of the catholic faction at court. His murder was in fact the result of a blood feud which had begun with the assassination of François, duke of Guise during the siege of Orléans in February 1563 and for which Coligny was held responsible by members of the Guise family. In a clumsy effort to cover the traces of Coligny's death, members of the catholic faction at court (with, it is now generally agreed, the complicity of the queen mother, Catherine de Médicis) tried to organize the elimination of other protestant leaders who were gathered in Paris for the wedding celebrations. This dangerous political manoeuvre got out of hand and was the beginning of the events known as the massacre of St Bartholomew. The 'bloody nuptials' of 1572 ended the attempts of the Huguenots to win the king's favour before 1589. After 1572, French protestants had to live with the memory of Coligny's assassination and the massacre which followed it.

Sectarian Violence

Edicts of pacification and court politics could do little to overcome the popular catholic hostilities provoked by the protestant church militant and nourished by political instability. The outbreaks of sectarian tension on the eve of the French civil wars were bloody, violent and unpredictable. The word 'massacre' in French (and then in English) – like the word holocaust in our own century – gained its particular, gruesome meaning of the ruthless slaughter of human beings from the French civil wars. Historians have still not analysed in full the evidence of, or found wholly convincing explanations for, this explosion of (largely urban) sectarian violence and the reactions it produced. The desire on the part of catholics to 'purify' their cities from the contagion of heresy was the natural reaction of those whose living space (invested, as we have seen, with the weight of religious tradition) had been 'polluted' by heresy (Davis, 1975, ch. vi). Without images or relics, protestants and their Bibles became the targets for ritual purification. This, in part, may explain why protestant bodies were mutilated, their ears cut off (*fricassée* of the ears of Huguenot victims was supposed to have been prepared by the catholic soldiers after the surrender of Orléans in 1563), their intestines sold and their genitalia removed. We should not ignore completely, however, the effects of economic hardship on these urban populations (there was a tendency for massacres to occur at times of high grain prices, although the correlation was not exact), or the incendiary atmosphere created when noblemen, used to imposing martial discipline, were faced with handling the highly charged circumstances of a city in revolt. The implacable marshal de Tavannes, royal lieutenant of Burgundy, for example, was reduced to tears of rage when a crowd of Huguenot women in Dijon challenged his authority in 1561. The civil wars added other dimensions to this popular violence – feud, hatred of foreigners, dislike between town and country, old scores and private quarrels, elements of class war, all appeared in the grotesque carnival-cum-massacre of Romans in 1580 (Le Roy Ladurie, 1980).

As protestants attacked catholic rituals, pulled down images, stained-glass, relics and otherwise offended or ridiculed objects of catholic veneration, they forcefully provoked the considerable, popular reserves of strength in local, often lay, catholicism (Galpern, 1976, ch. vi; Richet, 1977; Benedict, 1981, pp. 111–12). Processions and pilgrimages began again, to ensure that patron saints were assuaged. Commemorative crosses were erected; new miracles were reported. A hawthorn bush in the cemetery of the Holy Innocents in Paris spontaneously burst into flower at the beginning of the Paris massacres in 1572, while at Troyes in 1561 a copper cross (whose healing powers had apparently lapsed in the first half of the century) changed colour and began to cure people again at the start of sectarian disturbance in the town. Fraternities – traditional institutions for catholic laymen – were reformed too (Greengrass, 1984, p. 6). In May 1568, for example, over 400 people gathered in the ruined cathedral at Mâcon in Burgundy to swear an oath to the newly formed fraternity of the Holy Ghost and pledged to rebuild all the city's churches. Two months later, a Calvinist nobleman was killed outside his house there by masked men – the first fruits of the fraternity's malevolence, or so the admiral de Coligny claimed. Elsewhere there were local syndicates and leagues with distinctive badges and bonnets, which together made up the grassroots of the more organized catholic League of the 1580s, the climax of the French civil wars. Although not yet plumbed into the mains supply of the catholic counter-reformation, French catholicism continued to tap considerable streams of loyalty to the old religion to counter the protestants.

The St Bartholomew Massacre

Among the sectarian events of the civil wars, the massacre of St Bartholomew dwarfs the others in scale and significance. Beginning in Paris on the night of St Bartholomew's eve, Saturday 23 August 1572, the massacre of protestants lasted several days in the capital before spreading, like a contagion, to 12 major provincial cities. As Michelet said, it was not a day but a 'season', and latest estimates suggest a cautious figure of about 3,000 killed in Paris with another 8,000 elsewhere (Garrisson-Estèbe, 1973). The reactions of protestants were at the extremes of apoplectic rage, stupefaction and accusations of treachery. For Theodore Beza in Geneva, writing to a friend in Heidelberg in September, it was 'despair and distraction'; 'God have pity upon us. Never has the like of such perfidy and atrocity been seen. How many times have I predicted it! How many times have I averted it! God has let it happen, God who is justly angered; and yet he is our Saviour!' To noble protestants, the massacre was an offence against the values of aristocratic fidelity; the king had broken his word. To the protestant communities of the south and to the lawyers in the Huguenot cause, it was a royal treason, a gigantic felony, perpetrated without warning. Engagements had been solemnly undertaken by the monarchy in edicts of pacification; pledges of mutual respect were implied in the marriage of Henri of Navarre with the king's sister. All had been broken, as had protestant respect and trust in the monarchy. It did not take long for protestants to seek to explain what had happened as a premeditated catholic plot in which Catherine de Médicis was the wicked Italian queen, Charles ix her apprentice and his brother Henri (later Henri iii) her accomplice.

The massacre of St Bartholomew weakened allegiance to protestantism in many regions and localities, and pushed it back on to the defensive. Many of its most committed noble supporters – those who were in Paris for the royal nuptials – were eliminated and those who were not, fearing for their lives, sought a hasty refuge abroad or, out of necessity, made prudence a virtue and abjured. Surviving registers of protestant baptisms suggest that the massacre affected protestant affiliation quite severely everywhere, save for those stronghold cities such as Montauban, La Rochelle or Nîmes, where no other religion except protestantism was permitted (Benedict, 1981, ch. v). Catholic registers of abjurations began to be kept after this date, indicating a patchy and uneven erosion of individual protestant loyalties. Consistories became concerned with acts of recidivism, whether it was attending a catholic sermon or drinking with catholic friends; by the 1590s, in a survey of 15 consistory court records from the south of France, about 45 per cent of the cases heard by the courts concerned this problem (Garrisson-Estèbe, 1980, pp. 71–6).

The massacre also modified the political structure of the Huguenot movement, turning it back to its regional component parts and allowing, in the absence of a strong noble contingent, its political assemblies to have a greater say in its affairs (Garrisson-Estèbe, 1980, pp. 177–95). These were dominated by ministers and deputies from the towns of the Midi, who proved adept at putting together the necessary funds for military campaigns and continuing the civil wars. They abandoned the pretence of being the loyal servants of a king surrounded by tyrants and, whilst they did not make a great display of republican sentiments, they wore their royalism lightly in the 1570s. This is why they have been called the 'United Provinces of the Midi' during these years.

Continuing to fight the civil wars, however, had its costs for the protestant movement. Fighting the French monarchy was not easy; its tremendous resources, great institutional strengths and enormous powers of recuperation simply could not be matched by the protestant communities. The maintenance of churches and ministers, the contributions to the war, the costs of the Huguenot political structure, its deputies and assemblies, all placed a great burden on individual protestant families. In addition, the civil wars damaged, in some cases severely, the prospects for commercial activity in France, so that the relatively more secure investment in royal offices became much more attractive; but protestants were excluded from the most lucrative of these posts by virtue of their religion.

Above all, the mentality and outlook of French protestantism gradually changed as the events of St Bartholomew reinforced the effects which the civil wars had already had. A protestant church militant gradually became a protestant church under the cross, disciplined (the obedience shown to the consistory, despite its efforts fundamentally to change aspects of social behaviour, was remarkable), defensive and distrustful of royal authority. In 1562, Morély had called for a series of provincial histories of the reformed churches in France to give testimony to the triumph of congregations of the faithful under persecution (Morély, 1968, pp. 344–7). A year later, at the national synod of Lyon (which he may have attended), a proposal for a 'faithful record of all that is most remarkable which has occurred by Divine Providence' to the French churches was accepted and the various *colloques* were asked to prepare such histories (*Histoire ecclésiastique*, 1883, vol. iii, introduction). Twenty years later, they were collected and published in Geneva as the *Ecclesiastical History* of the reformed churches of France. But as the contributions from the various provinces had trickled in over the intervening years, it had changed from being a confident record of the gradual revelation of God's truth in France to an account of the mysterious and incomprehensible workings of providence for an embattled minority. The image used on the title-page was of three soldiers striking on the anvil of Truth with hammers (one of which is in the process of breaking). The legend round the woodcut ran simply: 'The more blows you use, the more hammers you lose' (*Plus a me frapper on s'amuse, Tant plus de marteaux on y use*). It was the dignified emblem of what was to become, in the next generation, a lost cause.

Appendix
The Social Geography of French Protestantism around 1560

The following statistics (see table 1) need to be treated with considerable caution. All social divisions imposed upon the evidence are to some extent arbitrary ones. They are based on relatively small samples and we have no way of measuring the extent to which protestantism reflected – or failed to – the social milieu of the places and regions from which these samples are taken.

Table 1   A social breakdown of French protestantism around 1560

	Clergy (%)	Seigneurs (%)	Liberal professions (%)	Merchants (%)	Artisans (%)	Agricultural workers (%)	Various (%)	Servants (%)
Suspects before the *Chambre Ardente* 1547–50[a]	34	4	13[h]	10	39	0	–	–
Suspects before the *parlement* of Toulouse 1510–60[b]	33	6	35.5[h]	8	17	0.5	–	–
Social status of French protestants registered in the *livre des Habitants*, Geneva 1549–60[c]	0	3	12	8	68.5	3.5	5	–
Toulouse protestants 1562–3[d]	0	4.6[g]	35.3	14.6	38.7	–	–	6.8
Montpellier protestants 1560[e]	0	2.3	15.4	8.5[i]	69	4.8	–	–
Grenoble protestants 1561–73[f]	0	5.1[g]	40.9	15.2	33.9	–	–	4.9

a Salmon, 1975. The sample is of 160 of the 312 suspects (51.2%).
b Mentzer, 1984, p. 152. The sample is of 424 of 1074 suspects (39.4%).
c Mandrou, 1959, p. 665. The sample is of 2247 from a total group of 4776 (47%).
d Davies, 1979, p. 38. The sample is of 681 out of 1127 suspects (60.4%).
e Le Roy Ladurie, 1974, p. 160. The sample analyses 561 of 817 (68%).
f Davies, 1979, p. 50. The sample is of 212 suspects.
g Including military.
h Including royal office holders.
i Including *bourgeois*.

References and
Further Reading

Those items which are asterisked guide students to accessible, recent literature, mainly in English, for further reading. Publishers are not cited for works before 1945.

Aubert, F. 1947: A propos de l'affaire de la rue Saint-Jacques (4–5 septembre 1557). *Bulletin de la société d'histoire du protestantisme français*, 73, 96–102.

Badouelle, G. (ed.) 1976: *Jacques Lefèvre d'Etaples ... Epistres et Evangiles pour le cinquante et deux dimenches de l'an*. Leiden: Brill.

*Benedict, P. 1981: *Rouen in the Wars of Religion*. Cambridge: Cambridge University Press.

Berthoud, G. (ed.) 1957: *Aspects de la propagande religieuse en France au XVIe siècle*. Geneva: Droz.

Berthoud, G. 1973: *Antoine Marcourt, réformateur et pamphlétaire ...* Geneva: Droz.

*Cameron, E. 1984: *The Reformation of the Heretics*. Oxford: Oxford University Press.

Chartier, R., Compère, M.M. and Julia, D. 1976: *L'Education en France du XVIe au XVIIIe siècles*. Paris: SEDES.

Chassin du Guerny, Y. and de Gennes, J.P. 1978: Les d'Airebaudouze d'Anduze. In J.D. Bergasse (ed.), *Hommage à Jacques Fabre de Morlhan*. Albi: l'OST, 211–26.

Chevalier, B. (ed.) 1985: *Histoire de Tours*. Toulouse: Privat.

Clive, H.P. 1983: *Marguerite de Navarre: An Annotated Bibliography*. London: Grant and Cutler.

'Coligny' 1974: *L'Amiral de Coligny et son temps*. Société de l'Histoire du protestantisme français.

Constant, J.-P. 1981: *Nobles et paysans en Beauce au XVIe et XVIIe siècles*. Doctoral thesis, University of Paris.

Croix, P. 1981: *La Bretagne aux 16e et 17e siècles: la vie, la mort, la foi*. 2 vols. Paris: Maloine.

*Davies, J.M. 1979: Persecution and protestantism: Toulouse, 1562–75. *The Historical Journal* 22, 31–51.

*Davis, N.Z. 1975: *Society and Culture in Early Modern France*. Stanford: Stanford University Press.

*Davis, N.Z. 1981: The sacred and the body social in sixteenth-century Lyon. *Past and Present*, 90, 40–70.

Degert, A. 1904: Procès de huit évêques français suspects de calvinisme. *Revue des questions historiques*, 61–108.

Delumeau, J. 1977: *Catholicism between Luther and Voltaire*. London: Burns and Oates.

Dewald, J. 1980: *The Formation of a Provincial Nobility*. Princeton: Princeton University Press.

Dez, P. 1936: *Histoire des protestants et des églises réformées de Poitou*. La Rochelle.

Dufour, A. 1963: L'affaire de Maligny vue à travers la correspondance de Calvin et de Bèze. *Cahiers d'histoire*, 8, 269–80.

*Farge, J.K. 1985: *Orthodoxy and Reform in Early Reformation France*: The Faculty of Theology of Paris, 1500–1543. Leiden: Brill.

Febvre, L. 1944: *Autour de l'Heptaméron; amour sacré, amour profane*. Paris.

*Febvre, L. 1969: *Au cœur religieux du XVIe siècle*. 2nd edn. Paris: SEVPEN.

Febvre, L. and Martin, H-J. 1976: *The Coming of the Book*. London: NLB.

Foisil, M. 1981: *Le Sire de Gouberville*. Paris: Aubier-Montaigne.

*Galpern, A.N. 1976: *The Religions of the People in Sixteenth-Century Champagne*. Cambridge, Mass.: Harvard University Press.

Garrisson, F. 1950: *Essai sur les commissions d'application de l'édit de Nantes*. Paris.

*Garrisson-Estèbe, J. 1973: *Tocsin pour un massacre*. Paris: Editions d'Aujourd'hui.

*Garrisson-Estèbe, J. 1980: *Protestants du Midi*. Toulouse: Privat.

Geisendorf, P. 1963: Métiers et conditions sociales du premier refuge à Genève, 1549–87. In *Mélanges Antony Babel*. Geneva: Droz, 239–49.

*Gilmont, J.-F. 1981: *Jean Crespin, un éditeur réformé du XVIe siècle*. Geneva: Droz.

Gray, J.G. 1983: The origin of the word Huguenot. *Sixteenth Century Journal*, 14, 349–59.

Greengrass, M. 1983: The anatomy of a religious riot in Toulouse in May 1562. *Journal of Ecclesiastical History*, 34, 367–91.

Greengrass, M. 1984: *France in the Age of Henri IV*. London: Longman.

Guggenheim, A.H. 1972: The calvinist notables of Nîmes during the era of the religious wars. *Sixteenth Century Journal* 3, 80–96.

Harding, R.R. 1978: *Anatomy of a Power Elite*. New Haven: Yale University Press.

Hauser, H. 1899: The French reformation and the French people. *American Historical Review*, 4, 217–27.

*Heller, H. 1977: Famine, revolt and heresy at Meaux, 1521–5. *Archiv für Reformationsgeschichte*, 68, 132–56.

*Higman, F. 1979: *Censorship and the Sorbonne*. Geneva: Droz.

Higman, F.M. (ed.) 1982: *Guillaume Farel: le Pater Noster et le Credo en françoys*. Geneva: Droz.

Higman, F.M. 1983: Luther et la piété de l'église gallicane; le *Livre de vraye et parfaicte oraison*. *Revue d'histoire et de philosophie religieuse*, 68, 91–111.

*Higman, F. 1984: Les traductions françaises de Luther, 1524–1550. In J.-F. Gilmont (ed.), *Palaestra Typographica*. Brussels, 11–56.

Histoire ecclésiastique 1883: 3 vols (eds) G. Baum and E. Cunitz. Paris.

Huppert, G. 1984: *Public Schools in Renaissance France*. Chicago: Illinois University Press.

Huseman, W.H. 1984: The expression of the idea of toleration in French during the sixteenth century. *Sixteenth Century Journal*, 15, 293–310.

*Imbart de la Tour, P. 1946: *Les origines de la réforme*. 4 vols. 2nd edn. Melun: Librairie d'Argences.

Jourda, P. 1930: *Répertoire analytique et chronologique de la correspondance de Marguerite d'Angoulême ...*. Paris.

Joutard, P. 1979: *Les Cévennes*. Toulouse: Privat.

*Kelley, D. 1973: *François Hotman: A Revolutionary's Ordeal*. Princeton: Princeton University Press.

*Kelley, D. 1981: *The Beginning of Ideology*. Cambridge: Cambridge University Press.

*Kingdon, R.M. 1956: *Geneva and the Coming of the Wars of Religion in France, 1555–1563*. Geneva: Droz.

*Kingdon, R.M. 1967: *Geneva and the Consolidation of the French Protestant Movement, 1564–1572*. Geneva: Droz.

*Knecht, R.J. 1978: Francis I, 'Defender of the Faith?'. In E. Ives, R.J. Knecht and J.J. Scarisbrick (eds), *Wealth and Power in Tudor England*. London: Athlone, 157–222.

*Knecht, R.J. 1982: *Francis I*. Cambridge: Cambridge University Press.

Lamet, M.S. 1978: French protestants in a position of strength in the early years of the reformation in Caen, 1558–1568. *Sixteenth Century Journal*, 9, 35–55.

Le Roy Ladurie, E. 1974: *The Peasants of Languedoc*. Illinois: Chicago University Press.

*Le Roy Ladurie, E. 1980: *Carnival: A People's Rising in Romans, 1579–80*. London: Scolar Press.

Livet, G., Rapp, F. and Rott, J. 1977: *Strasbourg au cœur religieux du XVIe siècle*. Strasbourg: Librairie ISTRA.

*Lloyd, H.A. 1983: *France, the State and the Sixteenth Century*. London: Allen and Unwin.

Lublinskaya, A.D. 1966: *Lettres et mémoires adressés au chancelier P. Séguier 1633–1649*. Moscow and Leningrad: Soviet Academy of Sciences.

McNeill, J.T. (ed.) 1961: *The Institutes of the Christian Religion*. 2 vols, Library of the Christian Classics. Philadelphia: The Westminster Press.

Mandrou, R. 1959: Les français hors de France aux XVIe et XVIIe siècles. *Annales: E.S.C.*, 14, 662–75.

*Mandrou, R. 1975: *Introduction to Early Modern France, 1500–1640*. London: Edward Arnold.

Mann, M. 1934: *Erasme et les débuts de la réforme française (1517–36)*. Paris.

Martin, H.-J. and Chartier, R. 1982: *Histoire de l'édition française*, vol. 1. Paris: Promodis.

*Mentzer, R. 1984: Heresy proceedings in Languedoc, 1500–1560. *Transactions of the American Philosophical Society*, 74.

Meyer, J.P. 1984: La Rochelle and the failure of the French reformation. *Sixteenth Century Journal*, 15, 169–83.

Meylan, H. and Dufour, A. (eds) 1976–: *Correspondance de Théodore de Bèze*. 9 vols. Geneva: Droz.

Mirouse, F. 1984: Devenir prêtre à Toulouse au XVe siècle; les ordinations du clergé séculier: 1482–97. *Bulletin de littérature ecclésiastique*, 85, 41–59.

*Molinier, A. 1984: Aux origines de la réformation cévenole. *Annales E.S.C.*, 39, 240–60.

Monter, E.W. 1967: *Calvin's Geneva*. New York: John Wiley.

*Monter, E.W. 1979: Historical demography and religious history in sixteenth-century Geneva. *Journal of Interdisciplinary History*, 9, 399–427.

Moore, W.G. 1930: *La Réforme allemande et la littérature française*. Strasbourg.

Morély, J. 1968: *Traité de la discipline et police chrestienne*. Geneva: Slatkine Reprints.

*Nicholls, D. 1980: Social change and early protestantism in France; Normandy, 1520–62. *European Studies Review*, 9, 279–308.

Nicholls, D. 1981: Inertia and reform in the pre-Tridentine French Church: the response to protestantism in the diocese of Rouen, 1520–62. *Journal of Ecclesiastical History*, 32, 185–97.

*Nicholls, D. 1982: The nature of popular heresy in France, 1520–42. *The Historical Journal*, 26, 261–75.

*Nicholls, D. 1984: The social history of the French reformation: ideology, confession and culture. *Social History*, 9, 25–43.

Pariset, J.-D. 1981: *Les relations entre la France et l'Allemagne au milieu du XVIe siècle*. Strasbourg: Librairie ISTRA.

*Parker, T.H.L. 1975: *John Calvin*. London: Darton and Todd.

Pineaux, J. 1971: *La poésie des protestants de langue française*. Paris: Klincksieck.

*Potter, G.R. and Greengrass, M. 1983: *John Calvin*. London: Edward Arnold.

Poujol, J. 1973: De la Confession de Foi de 1559 à la Conjuration d'Amboise. *Bulletin de la société d'histoire du protestantisme français*, 109, 158–77.

Raemond, F. de 1605: *Histoire de la naissance, du progrès et de la décadence de l'hérésie* ... Bordeaux.

Rapp, F. 1971: *L'Eglise et la vie religieuse en Occident*. Paris: Presses Universitaires de France.

*Renaudet, A. 1953: *Préréforme et humanisme à Paris pendant les premières guerres d'Italie (1494–1517)*. Paris: Librairie d'Argences (2nd edn).

Rice, E.F. 1972: The humanist idea of christian antiquity: Lefèvre d'Etaples and his circle. *Studies in the Renaissance*, 9, 126–60.

*Richet, — 1977: Aspects socio-culturelles des conflits religieux à Paris dans la seconde moitié du XVIe siècle. *Annales E.S.C.*, 32, 764–89.

*Roelker, N. 1968: *Queen of Navarre: Jeanne d'Albret*. Cambridge, Mass.: Harvard University Press.

Romier, L. 1913: *Les origines politiques des guerres de religion*. 2 vols. Paris.

*Romier, L. 1925: *Le Royaume de Catherine de Médicis: La France à la veille des guerres de religion*. 2 vols. Paris.

Rosenberg, D.L. 1978: *Social experience and religious choice: a case study, the protestant weavers and woolcombers of Amiens in the sixteenth century*. Ph.D. thesis, Yale University.

*Salmon, J.H.M. 1975: *Society in Crisis: France in the Sixteenth Century*. London: Benn.

Sutherland, N.M. 1962: *The French Secretaries of State in the age of Catherine de Medici*. London: Athlone.

*Sutherland, N.M. 1973: *The Massacre of St Bartholomew and the European Conflict, 1559–1572*. London: Macmillan.

*Sutherland, N.M. 1980: *The Huguenot Struggle for Recognition*. New Haven: Yale University Press.

*Sutherland, N.M. 1984: *Princes, Politics and Religion, 1547–89*. London: Hambledon.

Veissière, M. 1975–7: *Guillaume Briçonnet et Marguerite d'Angoulême, correspondance*. Geneva: Droz.

Veissière, M. and Moreau, B. 1980: Edition et mécénat dans le premier quart du XVIe siècle. *Revue française d'histoire du livre*, 6, 21–46.

Venard, M. 1968: Pour une sociologie du clergé du XVIe siècle: recherches sur le recrutement sacédotal dans la province d'Avignon. *Annales E.S.C.*, 23, 987–1016.

Wendel, F. 1942: *L'Eglise de Strasbourg: sa constitution et son organisation, 1532–1535*. Paris.

Index

of Luther risked being burned for heresy alongside Lutherans, as was the poor hermit of Livry outside Meaux in 1525. The Waldensians were called 'Lutherans' by the *parlement* of Provence in 1533 although they seem to have had little if any connection with the German reformer. When the Sorbonne sat down in 1544 to try to ban heretical works, it found itself issuing an index that was an extraordinary rag-bag of forbidden books, including works by Rabelais, Dolet, Erasmus, Lefèvre d'Etaples, as well as Luther, Calvin and Zwingli.

The position is complicated because those who were most attracted by what Luther or Zwingli wrote, avoided too overt a connection with other religious reformers outside France. Instead, they tended to stress their devotion to the gospel (*l'évangile*) of the true message of Jesus Christ, and, for the historian Imbart de La Tour, evangelism represented all those who wanted a reform along protestant lines but without wishing to establish a separate church in order to achieve it (1946, vol iii). We can best recreate some of the atmosphere of this group by looking at the language and themes of the early translations of Luther's writings in vernacular French, since these were the ones which most worried the authorities as likely to spread the word furthest.

At the latest count, there are 22 surviving printed editions known to bibliographers of the works of Luther translated into French before 1550 (Higman, 1984). Many were produced in the printing centres of the Rhineland in Basle and Strasburg and in Antwerp which had an established place in the French market; but a number of titles were also published by the remarkable Parisian printing house of Simon Dubois, which enjoyed the protection of the king's sister and moved to Angoulême in January 1529 to continue its activities without the harassment of the authorities in the capital (Berthoud, 1957, pp. 1–27). Generally speaking, they presented the principal doctrinal questions in Lutheranism, although they were anxious to avoid giving needless offence. The translation often altered the balance of the Lutheran original significantly in order to reduce controversy. They tended to be packaged in a relatively non-controversial way and to avoid becoming entangled in specific controversies about indulgences or the papacy. Their language was that of St Paul, faith, the Word,

grace and sin, with an additional emphasis on idolatry and superstition, coupled with the vocabulary of redemption, sacrifice (of Christ), light (of the Gospels) and resurrection.

One of the earliest was Guillaume Farel's presentation of the Lord's Prayer and the Creed (the latter mainly a Lutheran translation), published in Basle in August 1524 (Higman, 1982). Farel (1489–1565) was one of those remarkably restless individuals who always happen to be in the right place at the right time. He grew up in the Dauphiné Alps (historians have often generously allowed him a Waldensian heritage), was trained in the university of Paris, moved to Meaux to be a companion of bishop Briçonnet, but then returned to Dauphiné before leaving France for a wandering life in the Rhineland. He then went on to form part of the French populations, at various times, of Strasburg, Basle, Metz, Montbéliard, Neuchâtel, Lausanne and, finally, Geneva where he invited Calvin to join him in 1536. In an introduction to the book, Farel presented all the main themes of evangelism. The truth faith in Jesus Christ was being stifled by 'the great negligence of the shepherds'; 'God's flock had been badly instructed.' To stimulate a true faith, they needed the essential parts of Scripture simply expounded, particularly the Commandments and the Lord's Prayer. The work was for popular use by the 'congregation of the faithful'; it was not designed for 'a breakaway church'. But the exposition of the texts which followed was, of course, a clear statement of the Lutheran tenets of the preeminence of Scripture, of faith over works, and of the priesthood of all believers. It was reprinted the following year by a Parisian press which had close contacts in Basle under the title *The Prayer of Jesus Christ* (*l'Oraison de Jesuchrist*) (Higman, 1983, pp. 91–111). But this explicit presentation of the Lutheran message proved too hot to stomach in the wake of the events of 1525–6 and was watered down to become a part of the first edition of *The Book of True and Perfect Prayer* (*Livre de vraye et parfaicte oraison*) printed in 1528. On the title page was a famous woodcut depicting Christ on the Mount of Olives with the disciples sleeping at his feet. This was to be the most popular text of evangelical piety in France, if we may measure this from the fact that it was reprinted no less than 14 times between 1528 and 1545. All the signs are that, despite the difficulties in

Lodève in 1489 as one of those royal nominees. He would later succeed his father as abbot of the wealthy and prestigious Parisian abbey of St-Germain-des-Prés in 1507. During the reign of Louis XII, Briçonnet played an active part in delicate Franco-papal diplomacy during the critical period in 1510 when a possible rupture threatened the two courts over the council of Pisa. He showed every sign of enjoying the wealth and power with which his family, positions and connections had endowed him.

But he was not afraid of being a patron of change. His role in the reform of his Parisian abbey gave him a reputation which was enhanced by his patronage of the works of those scholars most influenced by the so-called 'pre-reform'. Among those who dedicated their works to him and, it may be presumed, had some good reasons to be grateful for his protection, were his one-time tutor Josse Clichtove, François Vatable, a student at the university of Paris and a resident at St-Germain whose brilliance as a Greek and Hebrew scholar later earned him a chair at the royal College when it was founded in 1530, Pierre Richard, the famous preacher from Troyes, and Jacques Lefèvre d'Etaples (Veissière and Moreau, 1980, pp. 21–46). When Briçonnet was in Rome on diplomatic business in 1516–17, it would not have been out of character for him to have associated with the reforming fraternity of the Oratory of Divine Love, whose notions very much mirrored his own.

Briçonnet had been appointed bishop of Meaux, a small weaving town 30 miles east of Paris, in December 1515. On his return from Rome, he visited each parish in the diocese and, beginning with an important diocesan synod in October 1519 in which he presented his views of pastoral responsibility, began the reform of his diocese which, in the course of the next six years, was to turn it into the laboratory for evangelism. Those in Paris who had enjoyed his discerning patronage were invited to become his disciples and they form what historians often refer to as the Meaux group (*cercle de Meaux*). Lefèvre d'Etaples was appointed manager of the hospital in Meaux in 1521 and later became Briçonnet's vicar general. Gérard Roussel and François Vatable accepted benefices in the town and later became canons in the cathedral. Famous preachers such as Martial Mazurier and promising young men like Guillaume Farel were invited to take part in evangelizing the diocese, following a novel arrangement which divided the parishes into 32 preaching circuits with each assigned a permanent and regular preacher. Parishes were encouraged to include the reading of the Epistles and the Gospels at the Mass which would then be expounded in short homilies. It was partly with this in mind that Lefèvre d'Etaples published anonymously his French translation of the Gospels, with evangelical glosses, in Paris in June 1523, with the remainder of the New Testament following five months later. In 1525, the famous *Epistles and Gospels for the 52 Sundays of the Year* (*Epistres et Evangiles pour les cinquante et deux dimenches de l'an*) appeared, prepared probably by Lefèvre with the collaboration of other members of the group, in which the homilies were printed alongside the text (Badouelle, 1976).

It is possible to speculate that Briçonnet might have been the one to lead and channel the energies which his experiment had released on a wider plane, and there were a few others (like bishop Sadoleto in the diocese of Carpentras) who were trying to do something along similar lines. But in reality, the evangelical reform in Meaux quickly attracted violently hostile criticism. The Franciscans of his diocese were incensed at being so comprehensively up-staged. Evangelical ideas took root among the weavers of the city where, as appears to be the case in the Low Countries, the bad harvest of 1521 and the subsequent famine of 1522 had encouraged popular protests against the venality of the traditional church (Heller, 1977, pp. 142–7). One Jean Le Clerc was whipped through the streets of Meaux for having put up posters attacking indulgences while his mother fortified him with the cry: 'Long Live Jesus Christ and his Disciples' (*Histoire ecclésiastique*, 1883, vol i, p. 14). Briçonnet hastily issued orders in October and December 1523 requiring his preachers to reaffirm the validity of Purgatory and the power of prayers to the Virgin Mary and the Saints, and revoking the licences of some preachers who were suspect of Lutheranism. Briçonnet's own prudence emerged in his letters to the king's sister. 'Scandal' was to be avoided at all costs; reform was, to him, a powerful drug which, if applied too strongly, would kill the patient. Bishops were purifying Angels sent to administer the dose in small measures. But the *parlement* and the Sorbonne were frightened and they moved in 1525 to clear the clusters of heresy in the diocese. Many of his disciples sought exile in Strasburg; a few weavers who had set themselves up as evangelists in other dioceses were picked up while the bishop himself faced interrogation before the judges. The Meaux experiment was over, Briçonnet disgraced, and his dream for a renewal of the traditional church in France at an end.

At first sight, it would be difficult to imagine a more shy, solitary and retiring individual than the small secular priest of obscure origins in Picardy, Jacques Lefèvre d'Etaples (*c*.1450–1537). He gave the impression of wanting nothing better than to spend his life cocooned in the library at St-Germain in Paris, pursuing his studies, teaching and searching for 'the nectar of the fathers' – texts from the classical and Christian heritage of Europe which could then be carefully edited and published to contribute to the renewal of Christendom (Rice, 1972, pp. 126–60). The first step in his ambitious programme was to cleanse the old medieval philosophy by establishing a proper reading of the texts of Aristotle, particularly his *Metaphysics*. With this in mind, he and like-minded scholars could then apply the same procedures to other classical texts and to the Church Fathers. They would then establish proper, critical editions that threw light on the concepts and language of the works of Origen, Jerome, Augustine and so on. Through them an upright and pious scholar, instructed in the ways of contemplation by Nicolas of Cusa and the 'divine' Dionysius (Denis the Areopagite), might ascend to the reading, studying and commenting on the Scriptures themselves. And from the Scriptures would come, not a 'science' or 'theology' (which was what the medieval schoolmen had created), but a 'wisdom' (*sapientia*) and 'piety' which could be taught as simple truths (*simplex veritas*) to the unlearned. The last thing Lefèvre would have wanted to be called was an intellectual.

Lefèvre was therefore an elderly man (approaching 60) when, in 1509, he published his first edition of the Scriptures, beginning with the Psalms, a beautiful edition in five columns each corresponding to the various versions of the text. Among the select band of Biblical scholars of early sixteenth-century Europe, this book was among the most admired. He followed it, three years later, with his commentaries on the Epistles of St Paul. These were much studied and appreciated by Luther, who thought that he had a better appreciation of the Pauline notion of grace than Erasmus. Erasmus admired his courage for publishing such things under the noses of the reactionary Sorbonne but he would have little understood what was to come. In 1517, Lefèvre systematically pulled apart the fragile evidence for the existence of the step-sisters of the Virgin Mary. 1523 saw the publication of his first translations of Scripture into vernacular French, and his translation of the whole Bible in this form appeared in 1530. It is hard for us to imagine what a radical step it must have been for a scholar like Lefèvre to depart from the Latin of Christendom, in which meanings were well defined, into the fluid and unformed medium of the vernacular. There is something admirably daring in this elderly man in his seventies arriving in Strasburg from Meaux in 1525 to be a part of the evangelical group, in exile there from France. But although he was a pioneer, and his Bible of importance to the development of the French reform, Lefèvre did not belong in the Strasburg world and was not a leader of the younger generation. From Guillaume Farel, his pupil, we have the touching memory of the two men, young and old, together in the shadows of the chapel at St-Germain. Lefèvre knelt long in prayer and adoration before the images, saying his Holy Offices, much to the impatience of Farel; in reply, the old man 'would often say that *God* would renew the world and that I would see it'. Lefèvre died in 1536 at the court of Marguerite d'Angoulême at Nérac, before his scriptural translations appeared officially on the Sorbonne Index, but not before suspicions as to his orthodoxy had reduced him to self-imposed silence.

Both Briçonnet and Lefèvre enjoyed at various times the support and protection of Marguerite de Valois, duchess of Angoulême as a result of her first marriage, and queen of Navarre after her second marriage in 1527 to Henri d'Albret. She was a remarkable lady of many talents who has attracted the attentions of innumerable scholars (an annotated bibliography published in 1983 listed over 700 items – excluding editions of her works – about her) (Clive, 1983). She was a